The Gift of Failure

The Gift of Failure

How to step back and
let your child succeed

JESSICA LAHEY

First published in the United States
in 2015 by HarperCollins Publishers,
195 Broadway, New York,
NY 10007, USA

Published in the United Kingdom
in 2015 by Short Books,
Unit 316, ScreenWorks, 22 Highbury Grove,
London, N5 2ER

10 9 8 7 6 5 4 3 2 1

A CIP catalogue record for this book
is available from the British Library.

ISBN: 978-1-78072-2443

Cover design by Andrew Smith
Printed at CPI Group (UK) Ltd, Croydon, CR0 4YY

For Benjamin and Finnegan

I know you all, and will awhile uphold
The unyoked humour of your idleness.
Yet herein will I imitate the sun,
Who doth permit the base contagious clouds
To smother up his beauty from the world,
That, when he please again to be himself,
Being wanted, he may be more wonder'd at,
By breaking through the foul and ugly mists
Of vapours that did seem to strangle him.
If all the year were playing holidays,
To sport would be as tedious as to work;
But when they seldom come, they wish'd for come,
And nothing pleaseth but rare accidents.
So, when this loose behaviour I throw off
And pay the debt I never promised,
By how much better than my word I am,
By so much shall I falsify men's hopes;
And like bright metal on a sullen ground,
My reformation, glittering o'er my fault,
Shall show more goodly and attract more eyes
Than that which hath no foil to set it off.
I'll so offend, to make offence a skill,
Redeeming time when men think least I will.

Prince Hal, Act I, Scene 2, Henry IV, Part I

CONTENTS

Introduction: how I learned to let go

PART I

FAILURE: A MOST VALUABLE PARENTING TOOL

PART II

LEARNING FROM FAILURE: TEACHING KIDS TO TURN MISTAKES INTO SUCCESS

PART III

SUCCEEDING AT SCHOOL: LEARNING FROM FAILURE IS A TEAM EFFORT

Introduction:

HOW I LEARNED TO LET GO

I became a parent and a secondary school teacher in the same year, and these twin roles have shaped the way I've raised my children and educated my students. During my first decade raising two boys and teaching hundreds of children, I began to feel a creeping sense of unease, a suspicion that something was rotten in the state of my parenting. But it was only when my elder child started secondary school that my worlds collided and the source of the problem became clear to me: today's overprotective, failure-avoidant parenting style has undermined the competence, independence and academic potential of an entire generation. From my vantage point at the front of a classroom, I'd long viewed myself as part of the solution, a champion of my students' intellectual and emotional bravery. However, as the same caution and fear I witnessed in my students began to show up in my own children's lives, I had to admit that I was part of the problem, too.

We have taught our kids to fear failure, and in doing so, we have blocked the surest and clearest path to their success. That's certainly not what we meant to do, and we did it for all the best and well intentioned reasons, but it's what we have done nevertheless. Out of love and desire to protect our children's self-esteem, we have bulldozed every uncomfortable bump and obstacle out of their way, clearing the manicured path we hoped would lead to success and happiness. Unfortunately, in doing so we have deprived our children of the most important lessons of childhood. The setbacks, mistakes, miscalculations and failures we have shoved out of our children's way are the very experiences that teach them how to be resourceful, persistent, innovative, and resilient citizens of this world.

As I stood in my classroom on the day of my personal epiphany, looking at the students before me and seeing my own parenting clearly for the first time, I resolved to do what I needed to do to guide both my children and my students back toward the path to competence and independence. The way isn't smooth, and the going certainly isn't easy, but that's kind of the point. We parents are going to have to step back, leave those scary obstacles lying in the road, and allow our children to face them head-on. Given our support, love, and a *lot* of restraint, our kids can learn how to engineer their own solutions and pave their way toward success that is truly of their own making.

The discomfort I'd been feeling in my own parenting had been growing for a while, but I could not put my finger on where I'd gone wrong. I read all the parenting blogs, from the austere to the zealous, and read books by the experts on how to raise happy, healthy children. However, as I watched my boys approach their teenage years, something was amiss. They were good, well-adjusted kids, but I couldn't shake the sense that when the time came for them to head out on their own and make their way in the world, they were ill-prepared. As long as they stayed inside the safe haven I'd created for them, they were confident and successful, but when forced to venture outside, would they know how to function? I'd so extensively researched, planned and constructed their comfortable childhoods that I'd failed to teach them how to adapt to the world on *its* terms.

I never meant to teach my children to be helpless or to fear failure, and a life of anxiety is certainly not what I envisioned for them. On the contrary, I thought my kids would grow up brave, in the sort

The discomfort I'd been feeling in my own parenting had been growing for a while, but I could not put my finger on where I'd gone wrong.

of wild, free idyll I experienced as a child. I wanted them to explore the woods with a pocket knife and a couple of cookies shoved in their pockets, build tree houses, shoot handmade arrows at imaginary enemies, and swim in the local river. I wanted them to have the time and the courage to try new things, explore their boundaries, and climb one branch beyond the edge of their comfort zones.

But somehow, somewhere, that idyllic version of childhood morphed into something very different: a high-stakes, cut-throat race to the top. Today, careless afternoons in the woods seem like a quaint throwback because the pressure to succeed from an early age has ramped up for both parents and kids. There is no longer room in our children's schedules for leisure time in the woods, let alone opportunities to problem-solve their way out of the muck and mire they encounter out there. In the new normal, every moment counts, and the more successful our kids are as students, athletes and musicians, the more successful we judge ourselves as parents. The race to the top starts when children take their first steps and does not end until a five or sixfigure income is secured. And, come on, what kind of negligent mother allows her kids to play alone in the woods during homework time, with pockets full of sugar, armed to the teeth with pocket knives and arrows?

Modern parenting is dictated by fear. We bring a beautiful, precious child into the world, and after those first moments of bliss wear off, we realise that our new purpose in life is to protect this fragile human being from harm. And if we are to believe the fear-mongering mass media, that harm is all around us. Baby snatchers disguised as maternity nurses, antibiotic-resistant germs, toxic chemicals, disease-carrying ticks, bullying kids, unfair teachers, lurking paedophiles... no wonder we've all become anxious parents.

However, this fear doesn't just cause us to over-parent; it makes us feel overwhelmed. It's too hard to evaluate all the risks. It's easier to focus on trying to protect our kids from all threats, whether real or imagined, and when we tuck our kids in bed at night, free of cuts, bruises, or emotional hurt, we have, for one more day, found tangible evidence of our parenting success.

We reassure ourselves that there's plenty of time to teach them how to deal with risk and failure. Maybe tomorrow I'll let them walk to school, but today, they got to school safely. Maybe tomorrow they will do their own homework, but today, they are successful in math. Maybe tomorrow continues until it's time for them to leave home and by then, they have learned that we will always be there to save them from themselves.

I am as guilty as the next parent; I have inadvertently extended my children's dependence in order to feel good about my parenting. Every time I pack my child's lunch for him or drive his forgotten homework to school, I am rewarded with tangible proof of my conscientious mothering. I love, therefore I provide. I provide, therefore I love. While I know, somewhere in the back of my mind, that my children really should be doing these kinds of tasks for themselves, it makes me feel good to give them these small displays of my deep, unconditional love. I reassure myself with what feels like a vast expanse of childhood, stretching out for years, its eventual end invisible over the horizon. My kids will have their entire lives to pack their lunches and remember their school bags, but I only have a very brief window of time to be able to do these things for them.

There's a term for this behaviour in psychiatric circles. It's called enmeshment, and it's not healthy for children or parents. It's a maladaptive state of symbiosis that makes for unhappy, resentful parents and "failure to launch" children who move back in to their bedrooms after university. In 2012, 36% of 18-31 year-olds in the US were living their parents (this tallies with the trend in the UK, where in 2013 26% of 20-34 year-olds were living at home, a 25% increase since 1996). While some of that figure may be due to increased housing costs and declining marriage statistics, these numbers are part of a trend that's been rising for decades. In order to raise healthy, happy kids who can begin to build their own adulthood separate from us, we are going to have to extricate our egos from our children's lives and allow them to feel the pride of their own accomplishments as well as the pain of their own failures.

Decades of studies and hundreds of pages of scientific evidence point to one conclusion that sounds crazy, but it absolutely works: if parents back off the pressure and anxiety over grades and achievement and focus on the bigger picture – a love of learning and independent inquiry – grades will improve and test scores will go up. Children of controlling and directive parents are much less able to deal with intellectual and physical challenges than peers who benefit from parents who stand back and allow their children to try, and fail, and try again. Furthermore, the failure our children experience when we allow them to make their own mistakes is not only a necessary part of learning; it's the very experience that teaches them how to be resilient, capable, creative problem-solvers.

My flash of insight had been a long time coming. Yes, I'd been uncomfortable with my own over-parenting for a while, but I have to credit my students (again) for teaching me what I was too blind to see. Each year, my thirteen-year-old students write essays about an experience that has shaped their education, and after much struggle, one of my most tightly wound and anxiety-ridden students handed in the following paragraph:

> Some people are afraid of heights, some are afraid of water; I am afraid of failure; which, for the record, is called atychiphobia. I am so afraid of failing that I lose focus on what actually matters: learning. In focusing on the outcome, I lose the value of the actual assignment and deprive myself of learning.

She went on to recount all the ways this fear has held her back in school and athletics, but those first few sentences stopped me cold. Her experience as a student, my professional experience with her parents, my own parenting, and my son's fears all came together in her admission. This student's parents are wonderful, kind and caring, and they never intended to create this sort of fear in their child. And frankly, the fallout would be their own problem to deal with save for the fact that the private choices parents make that undermine their child's social, academic, and emotional development eventually come into conflict with a teacher's ability to educate their child.

Now that I understand the root cause of parents' fears and worries, I do what I can to convince them that a small blip in their child's journey means so little in the big picture and can actually serve as a great opportunity to teach their child about resilience. In order to help children make the most of their education, parents must begin to relinquish control and focus on three goals: embracing opportunities to fail, finding ways to learn from that failure, and creating positive home-school relationships. In the chapters that follow, I'll explain each of these goals in depth and give you strategies that will help you achieve them.

The day I finally came to terms with my over-parenting, I was determined to start making amends at home with my own children. I needed to do something immediate, something symbolic, and I knew just where to start. My younger son, then aged nine, had never learned to tie his shoes. I blamed this oversight on the invention of Velcro and his preference for slip-on shoes, but if I'm completely honest, I knew I was falling down on the job. He freaked out when I mentioned the situation, even in my most enthusiastic "Won't this be a fun project we can do together?"

voice. He got frustrated with my instruction, I got frustrated with his helplessness, and the entire endeavour dissolved into anger and tears. Tears. Over *shoelaces*. When I began to look closely at the source of his issue with the shoelaces, I realised that what he was feeling – the frustration and helplessness – was my fault, not his. I had taught him that.

For every time I tied his shoes, rather than teach him to do it himself, I reinforced his perception that I believed the task was too hard for him. Eventually he and I both began to wonder whether he'd ever prevail. One day before school, when he'd left his Velcro shoes at a friend's house and had to wear the back-up pair with laces, he said he'd rather wear his wellington boots than try to tie his shoes. He didn't even care that wearing boots meant he'd have to sit out PE all by himself.

This, right here, is what I had brought about: my son was so convinced of his inability that he was willing to forfeit an hour of games with his friends.

So that afternoon, I took out his back-up trainers, and prepared to remedy the situation. Over a snack, I told him I'd made a mistake and that I thought I'd figured out how to be a better mum. I empathised with his worry and told him that while the task might be hard for him at first, with some effort and perseverance, I knew he could conquer it. I was so confident he would, that we were going to stick with it until he mastered those darn shoelaces. In less than an hour, the embarrassment he'd felt about being the only child in his year who could not tie his shoes was gone. He had succeeded and I've hardly ever seen him so proud of himself. All it took was a little time, a little faith in each other, and the patience to work through the tangle of knots and loops.

No, it's not always going to be this simple. The stakes get higher and the consequences get bigger as our children get older. Lumpy knots and uneven shoelaces give way in the blink of an eye to flawed university dissertations and botched job interviews, and there's only so much time available to instill confidence and resilience in our children. The work begins the first moment our babies fail to grasp a toy or fall as they toddle across the room, and continues until they head out into their own lives. The sooner parents learn to appreciate the positive aspects of hardship and allow children to benefit from the upside of failure in childhood, the sooner all of us will have the opportunity to share in the moments of pride like the one I saw on my son's face as he secured those laces.

It's up to us. Parents have the power to grant this freedom to fail. Teachers have the ability to transform that failure into an education. And together? Together, we have the potential to nurture a generation of confident, competent adults.

Let's get started.

Part I

Failure: A Most Valuable Parenting Tool

1

HOW FAILURE BECAME A DIRTY WORD: A BRIEF HISTORY OF WESTERN PARENTING

As a child, I was obsessed with the *Little House on the Prairie* books. I wanted to live in a sod dugout on the banks of Plum Creek or a tiny cabin in the Big Woods under the strict but loving guidance of Ma and Pa Ingalls. I wanted to be Laura, who bravely roamed the dangerous and exciting world around her and made plenty of mistakes as she made her way across the prairie. When she returned home to face the music, her parents responded not with anxiety and fear, but with interest in her adventures and an eye toward her education in the great big beyond.

I strove to be tolerant of my sister, just as Laura was of Carrie. When the extravagant gift I coveted did not appear under our Christmas tree, I reminded myself of the year Laura received only a small tin cup, a piece of candy, a small cake, and a penny, and tried to be grateful. Remnants of

my "What would Laura do?" mentality survived into adulthood, and I could not wait to read the *Little House* books
to my own children, to teach them about Laura's world
of clear-cut morality and balloons made of pig bladders.
We read and relived their favourite moments – dribbling
syrup on snow to make candy, colouring butter with the
juice of grated carrots, and tracing patterns in the window
frost with a thimble. I encouraged them to wander our
Not-So-Big Woods; even as I worried about their safety, I
did my best to be that reassuring, firm and loving Ma for
my sons.

Ma and Pa set clear limits and goals for their children.
Right was right, wrong was wrong, learning arose from
failure, and when parents had to discipline, consequences
were swift and just. And so, when I became a parent, "What
would Laura do?" became "What would Ma do?" and I
continue to strive to raise my children according to that
ideal. I try to remember that their mistakes and failures are
a necessary and inevitable part of their growing up.

The fact that I turn to the late nineteenth century for
advice says a lot about how complex and confusing parenting has become. Ma and Pa understood that the job of a
parent is to raise self-sufficient, capable and ethical adults.
I envy their clarity, because sometimes, I'm not sure what
my job is. One day it is to be my son's friend so he will feel
comfortable enough to confide in me, the next it is to stand
firm as an authority figure and teach him to write thankyou
notes whether he wants to or not.

If I'm confused by my role, he must be, too. No wonder
I yearn for the simplicity of parenting in the Big Woods. I
fear, however, that even capable Ma and Pa Ingalls would be
overwhelmed and bewildered by the shifting expectations
and lack of solid footing in today's parenting landscape. In

order to get our bearings in this confusing territory, to understand how we arrived in this state of confusion, we need to find the signal in the noise of our collective parenting history.

Parenting in a simpler time

Parenting in Colonial New England was simpler in terms of its hierarchy of needs, defined as it was by risk and loss. Parents could expect to lose one in every ten children, even in the healthiest and wealthiest communities. In cities such as Boston, where urban poverty and close living quarters facilitated the spread of disease, childhood deaths were two to three times higher. When disaster struck, as it did during the 1677 smallpox epidemic, a fifth of the population died, most of them children. Parents to whom the sight of a dead child was "a sight no more surprising than a broken pitcher" were preoccupied with basic needs – the daily struggle for shelter, food, and safe drinking water – rather than the education, social life and emotional health of their children. Reason, rather than emotion, dominated early American childrearing. The voice of parenting philosophy in Colonial America, as far as such a thing existed, was that of John Locke. Where today we explain why it's not nice to bite the lady next door via a long-winded treatise accompanied by a supplicatory lollipop, Locke favoured a simpler solution, one that stressed clearheaded reason over emotion, for "[l]ong discourses and philosophical reasonings at best amaze and confound, but do not instruct children." Children were meant to be seen and not heard, and to always behave in the best interest of the family. They certainly were not allowed to make a scene. Toddler temper tantrums in the 1690 equivalent of the grocery store? Please. Locke advises "crying is very often a striving for mastery and an open declaration of their insolence or obstinacy: when they have not the power to obtain their desire, they will by their *clamor* and *sobbing* maintain their title and right to it" (emphasis Locke's, and I can almost hear the derision dripping from those *horrid, emotional* words). When children faced hardship and the consequences of their mistakes, Locke advised parents, "by no means bemoan them. This softens their minds and makes them yield to the little harms that happen to them, whereby they sink deeper into that part which alone feels, and makes larger wounds there than otherwise they would." In other words, correct and comfort, but do not pity or make a big deal out of children's hardship and failures because "the many inconveniences this life is exposed to require [that] we should not be too sensible of every little hurt." Locke was very much in favour of encouraging children to get back up and try again when they failed. "In the little harms they suffer from knocks and falls, they should not be pitied for falling, but bid do so again; which, besides that it stops their *crying* is a better way to cure their heedlessness and prevent their tumbling another time than either chiding or bemoaning them. But let the hurts they receive be what they will, [it will] stop their *crying* and that will give them more quiet and ease at present and harden them for the future" (again, the emphasis and disdain are Locke's). Colonial parents loved their children, and I'm sure they comforted them when they "suffered knocks and falls," but these obstacles were considered a part of daily life as one contributed, quietly and obediently, to the survival of the family in a harsh and dangerous land. Children grew up surrounded by the ups and downs of life and parents had more to focus on than the happiness of their offspring around the clock.

Parents pushed their children out of the nest much earlier in life than we do today. In the words of writer and Anglo-American revolutionary Thomas Paine, "Nothing hurts the affections, both of parents and children, so much, as living too closely connected, and keeping up the distinction too long." Children married young, had their own children soon after, and had to be ready to maintain their own trade, farms, and households before they left what we consider middle adolescence, so parents were under pressure to pass down an education in survival and independence from a very early age.

The American Revolution saw the birth of a new nation and a new philosophy regarding the nature of children and their place in family and society. Just as America rebelled against the rule of an English king who required blind allegiance and submission, writers and thinkers promulgated an analogous vision for American children. As Steven Mintz points out in his book *Huck's Raft: A History of American Childhood*, this move toward individuality can be illustrated by the concurrent shift in baby naming conventions. Until the American Revolution, children were typically named after a parent or a close relative in order to reinforce the significance of lineage and honour for the family. By the mid-eighteenth century, however, American parents began to bestow unique names on their children, sometimes paired with a middle name in an added display of individuality. Other customs that paid service to political, social, and familial hierarchies, such as children bowing to their parents, fell out of favour and the spirit of revolution began to seep into the minds and habits of a citizenry who refused to view themselves as subjects of any master, political or otherwise. Americans began to look toward the future of their new country, a nation of educated citizens that depended on children who would not bend to tyranny but value individual rights in service to freedom.

Despite the promise and heady idealism of this hard-won American independence, children still lived lives of quiet desperation. Up to half of all children lost a parent before they reached marriageable age, so many carried the weight of their own childhood work, as well as the work of a parent, on their narrow shoulders. Farm children as young as five were put to work and expected to do their share in order to secure their family's future. In cities, children had household chores, learned trades, and helped with the piecemeal work families brought into the home in order to earn extra money, such as laundry and sewing.

By the end of the nineteenth century, as the population and its economy moved away from the farm and toward the city, one out of every six children between ten and fifteen was employed. Mills and factories employed children because of their handy, compact size. They could squeeze their small bodies under industrial machinery in order to free snags and malfunctions, and they were a cheap and expendable form of labour.

The early part of the twentieth century marked a new awareness of the danger and horrors children endured in the workforce. Unsafe child labour practices led to the creation of child labour laws that prevented children below a certain age from working outside the home. Just as child labour was outlawed, mandatory school attendance became the law of the land. Children who used to work for the financial security of the family were now occupied with the work of education. These reforms were wonderfully beneficial, but from the perspective of the family and a society that measured a child's worth by his utility, children had become superfluous, and over the course of a generation, were transformed from "useful to useless," profitable to priceless. As more children were born and raised into a life of leisure, parents were left to cobble together new parenting goals in order to raise these very expensive, non-productive offspring.

The rise of the parenting expert

By the time *Parents* magazine appeared on news stands in 1926, the debate over parenting philosophy had taken hold in American culture and parents were eager for advice and information on how to raise their children in an increasingly confusing century. The era of the parenting expert had begun with the New Zealand health reformer Dr Truby King who published his influential book, *Feeding and Care of Baby*, in Britain in 1913. It sold 20,000 copies in five years and signalled a lapse in Western society's faith in the competence of parents. Where childrearing had once been absorbed into the fabric of everyday life, it now became a full-time job, requiring expert advice and training. Society no longer viewed children as miniature adults, capable of work and resourceful problem-solving, but vulnerable dependents requiring a great deal of well-researched and precise care. As the number of children per family shrank over the years, parents focused more on the individual child's emotional and psychological needs. All those idle children had time to express their psychological issues, and new theories of developmental psychology emerged to address those issues. Behaviours that would have been described in judgmental terms by John Locke were deemed emotional conditions to be treated rather than irritating behaviour to be corrected. Gone were the days of the sturdy, resilient child; the era of emotionally dependent children and anxious parents was officially under way.

Parents heard the message of late nineteenth and early-twentieth century experts loud and clear: mothers had no business raising a child without the advice of doctors. Women used to counsel other women on childrearing, gathering advice in the form of wisdom handed down over generations, but as pediatric medicine emerged as a specialty, the wisdom of generations past was treated with distrust, if not overt disdain. These experts advised women to turn a "deaf ear" to "the grandmother... [whose] influence is particularly pernicious, as she is supposed by her previous experience to know everything about babies." Before the twentieth century, parents (mostly mothers) took care of children's health care needs at home. Mothers kept a medical text, such as William Buchan's *Domestic Medicine*, in the home, and functioned as doctor, therapist, dentist, and teacher for their own children. At the turn of the century, however, the number of books on childrearing and child care exploded and, more significantly, their tone changed. Parenting had become a field of study and the experts writing the curriculum for this postgraduate specialty had little faith that mothers could succeed on their own.

The 1920s also marked the emergence of professional child care. Nursery schools were increasingly used as a way to educate all those ignorant mothers on the latest scientific advances in parenthood. Dependence on childrearing books, manuals, pamphlets and professionals was strongly encouraged, and an avalanche of these publications emerged. They were full of the advice about how to keep children safe from the threat of germs (another popular topic thanks to the discovery of the germ theory in the late nineteenth century) and attend to their children's ever-changing and newly pressing emotional needs, concerns that would have been laughable to parents just fifty years before. The mental and emotional state of children was a novel concept, and the "psychologising of childrearing" implied that parenting was not instinctual but a skill to be studied and learned. The consequences of improperly parenting a child included grave psychological damage and emotional distress, leading to syndromes such as sibling rivalry, phobias, sleeping disorders and teenage rebellion. Freud had popularised the theory of psychosexual development and warned parents about the dangers of neuroses due to improper toilet training, heaping the

> At the turn of the century, the number of books on childcare exploded and, more significantly, their tone changed. Parenting had become a field of study and the experts writing the curriculum for this postgraduate specialty had little faith that mothers could succeed on their own.

burden of adult psychological illness on improper mothering. Psychologist John Bowlby alerted parents about the serious harm that could result from incomplete attachment to our children; if we did not hold them enough, they would become maladapted juvenile delinquents. Children increasingly became the focus of their parents' lives, and by the time the fifties rolled around, the Western world had become fixated on the care, feeding and entertainment of its young.

Full faith and credit in experts persisted until a certain warm and fuzzy physician gave parents permission to trust themselves again.

You know more than you think you do

Dr Benjamin Spock's *Common Sense Book of Baby and Child Care*, published in 1946, sold ¾ million copies worldwide in its first year, and marked a shift in the tone parenting experts adopted when handing out advice. Dr Spock's book began with the shocking yet somehow comforting assurance, "Trust yourself," and "You know more than you think you do." With those introductory sentiments, he handed power back to parents. He hoped to halt our nation's over-dependence on experts, and it seemed he might just be the saviour of reason. Women still turned to doctors and psychologists for consultation, but Dr Spock, through his gentle tone and comprehensive manual, encouraged parents to exercise common sense and ownership of their parenting. While many found Spock's vote of confidence in parents a step back toward sanity, some people – experts who were losing their authority and parents who were frightened by the sudden lack of direction – found this freedom anxiety-provoking. Vestiges of antiquated theories about the fragility of infants and the lifelong impact of bad parenting decisions remained, and when these were paired with a new freedom from the inflexible instructions of experts, many parents were paralysed by the fear of their own power to tragically and irreversibly screw up their kids. As the fifties came to a close, a generation of children bent on rebellion and anti-establishment sentiment gave those experts plenty of ammunition in the case against Dr Spock's brand of feel-good parenting.

The 1960s exploded in bursts of social and political activism and its children began to believe in the power of a younger generation to change the world. John F. Kennedy, the youngest US president ever elected, succeeded the oldest, and the civil rights movement gained energy and momentum thanks to a generation of young activists. They were loud, they were gaining power, and there were simply more of them than ever before; the baby boom following World War II reduced the median age of the Western population to less than twenty years old. Adulthood, and the responsibility that came with it, lost its allure, and "power" lost its positive connotation as this younger generation was urged to actively question, rather than blindly follow, authority. Adolescence became a time of rebellion, experimentation and the search for identity, and now thanks to a combination of prolonged schooling, delayed marriage and jobs made scarce in a weak economy, it expanded further and further into what had traditionally been seen as adulthood. Consequently, adults who had been raised in a more authoritarian era, operating under the long-standing assumption that adulthood began at eighteen, felt increasingly powerless. Many parents put their hands up in defeat, and the media jumped on these parents for their overly permissive childrearing. Remember, child psychologists still espoused the theory that parents were likely responsible for the misdeeds of their children, particularly if they mucked up their child's infancy, so it made perfect sense that the media blamed parents for the historically unprecedented rebellion of the world's children. Permissive parents were labelled neglectful parents, as illustrated in Jules Henry's 1963 study, *Culture Against Man*, in which Henry pinned the blame for the insolence and insensitivity of America's adolescents on "the overly intense child-centered postwar family [that] produced children who found it difficult to break the umbilical cord during adolescence."

In the meantime, the family was falling apart, at least relative to what remained of the nostalgic glow of the 1950s. In Britain in particular, a whole series of events changed women's lives, starting with the introduction of the contraceptive pill in 1961. From 1964 married women were allowed to own and inherit property, which gave some women financial independence for the first time. New universities opened, and quotas on the number of places allowed to women began to be abolished. Better educated, more confident women demanded equal pay and equal rights. In the following decades divorce rates and cohabitation increased, and the age at which people started families began to rise.

As older, more independent and self-assured parents finally settled down to have children, they parented according to the attachment method, the natural extension of Spock's "Trust yourself" sentiment. Attachment parenting sought to strengthen the parent-child bond through constant, close contact and nurture. The idea was that strong bonds established in infancy persist over a lifetime. At the same time, the work of John Bowlby, strengthened public sentiment about the importance of attachment parenting and by 1989 when stories of Romanian orphanages hit our screens the theory of attachment parenting had become a dire warning: wear your children in a sling 24/7 or risk attachment disorder like those Romanian babies.

However, this message was incompatible with the reality most parents faced in the 1970s and 1980s. Women flooded the workforce in the wake of the feminist movement and were finally beginning to fulfil – and be recognised for – their potential as thinkers, innovators and leaders. More significantly, as inflation soared and recession settled in after the economic expansion of the 1960s, women *had* to work, and found themselves increasingly torn between the needs of home and jobs, children and financial security, attachment parenting and the psychological need to throw off the restrictive labels of motherhood and expand their rights as individuals.

Hence, mothers were fertile ground for seeding the self-esteem movement of the 1970s. Nathaniel Branden's 1969 book, *The Psychology of Self-Esteem*, kicked the movement off with a bang. His message, that self love is vital to emotional health, and that a person's self-evaluation "is the single most significant key to his behaviour," appealed to parents who sought to assuage their guilt in the face of so many conflicting demands. The individual, and his or her sense of self-worth, eclipsed the value of community or family. Nathaniel Branden envisioned a world in which children so valued themselves that the opinions of others would bounce off like some self-esteem force field, and we'd all live in a state of blissful self-exploration, self-satisfaction and self love. Unfortunately that's not quite how it worked out.

A generation of narcissists

Jean Twenge and W. Keith Campbell place the blame for *The Narcissism Epidemic* squarely on the back of the self-esteem movement. According to Twenge and Campbell, the result of this movement is not happier, healthier citizens; it is a generation of self-admiring narcissists focused on superficial appearances and personal gain, the "loadsamoney" culture with its emphasis on individual happiness and distrust of collective action and government.

The self-esteem movement promised that we could feel good about ourselves in everything we do, that children would always like their parents, and that we would feel great about our parenting all the time. But this is not how life – let alone effective parenting – works. Children who like their parents all the time tend not to be children who are corrected when they misbehave, or asked to consider the needs of other people. It does not *feel* good to punish or correct our children; no one wants to be the cause of tears and hurt feelings. It *feels* great to give our children sweets just before dinner with a conspiratorial finger over the lips, bonding with them in a shared, secret treat. It *feels* wonderful to swoop in and rescue them from detention and the stern glare of a teacher when we take that forgotten homework to school. The catch is that what *feels* good to us isn't always what *is* good for our children. We are not used to putting off what feels right and good for us in the short term in order to do what is right and good for our children in the long term.

The lure of short-term happiness and permissive, feel-good parenting became even more tempting as we heaped on guilt over increasing divorce rates, more hours spent at work, and less time spent with our children. Treats were traded for time together. When we did have time for them, we wanted to spend it in relative peace, not in squabbling over rules and consequences. It takes longer to teach a child how to clean a toilet than to clean the toilet ourselves, and time was short. I'm as guilty as anyone. My children are quite limited in their ability to cook, simply because I want and need that time in my kitchen to myself. It is my refuge from a day spent in the classroom or in doing things for my own children. I'll teach them how to cook someday, just not today.

As we move through this new millennium, parents are caught in a bit of a catch22. We are expected to feel good about ourselves and our parenting as we raise our children naturally and intuitively, while poring over more parenting books and magazines than at the same time about how to raise smart and creative and empathetic children who practise piano on their own, sleep nine hours a night and excel at school. We are expected to take up the mantle of those authoritarian experts we abandoned in the fifties and function as professionals both at home and at work. But then, at the sametime, as we sift through the reams of parenting advice, we are left to strike our own balance between work and home, and somehow trust our instincts as well as the experts. Today, parenting is less oxytocin-soaked rosy glow, more adrenaline-fuelled oncoming-headlight glare.

According to a post on *Parenting* magazine's website about today's most pressing parenting questions, we are concerned with the minutiae of parenting, such as "Will I spoil my baby if I pick her up every time she cries?" and "My baby does not reach his motor milestones as quickly as other infants do. Should I be worried?" Our focus has shifted from matters of life and death to the small details of children's mental, physical and emotional development, and the truth is that when we beg for answers to all those other nitpicky, insignificant questions, what we really want to know is "How will I know if I am a good parent?"

The answer, for most of us, is found in the moments when parenting feels good. I feel good when my children are safe, warm and fed, of course, but what really feels good, what makes me feel like an A-plus parent, is when I show my kids I love them by rescuing them from disappointment. Those times when I remember to pick up a book from the library I know my son will like, or when I show up at the last second before a football game with a forgotten mouthguard, reassure me that, "Yes, you *are* a good parent today."

Most of my adult life has been dedicated to the work of raising my children and until recently, that meant I spent my life protecting them from failure, all wrapped up in the safety of my loving embrace. But that's not working for us anymore, and it's certainly not working for my students and their families. I was afraid to abandon what felt good, afraid to put my needs aside and expose my children to the parts of life that hurt a little. Afraid I wouldn't hear my inner "Yes, you *are* a good parent today" anymore.

And yet the self-esteem movement is a failure, and doing what *feels* good has fostered a generation of narcissistic, self-indulgent children unwilling to take risks or cope with consequences. So what would be a better way? What parenting practice can help our children acquire the skills, values, and virtues on which a positive sense of self is built?

Parenting for autonomy. Parenting for independence and a sense of self, born out of real competence, not misguided confidence. Parenting for resilience in the face of mistakes and failures. Parenting for what is right and good in the final tally, not for what feels right and good in the moment. Parenting for tomorrow, not just for today.

2

WHY PARENTING FOR DEPENDENCE
DOESN'T WORK

I've known the mother sitting in front of me for years, and we have been through a lot together. I have taught three of her children, and I like to think we've even become friends during our time together. She's a conscientious mother who loves her children with all her heart. I've always been honest with her about their strengths and weaknesses, and I think she trusts me to tell her the truth. But when she hits me with the question that's been bothering her for a while, all I can do is nod and stall for time.

"Marianna's grades are fine; I'm not worried about that, but she just doesn't seem to love learning anymore."

She's absolutely right. I'd noticed the same thing about her daughter over the previous two or three years, and I have an answer, right there on the tip of my tongue, for what has gone wrong. Yet I'm torn between my responsibility to help Marianna and the knowledge that what I have to say is a truth I'm not sure this mother is ready to hear.

The truth – for this parent and so many others – is this: Marianna has sacrificed her natural curiosity and love of learning at the altar of achievement, and it's our fault... her parents, her teachers, society at large. We are all implicated in this crime against learning. From her first day of school, we pointed her toward that altar and trained her to measure her progress toward that goal by means of points, scores and awards. We taught her that her potential is tied to her intellect, and her intellect is more important than her character. We taught her to come home proudly bearing A's, championship trophies and university offers and we inadvertently taught her that we don't really care how she obtains them. We taught her to protect her academic and extra-curricular perfection at all costs and that it's better to quit when things get challenging than risk marring that perfect record. Above all else, we taught her to fear failure, and that fear has destroyed her love of learning.

I look at this mother with concern on her face, her eager pencil poised to write down my words of wisdom, and struggle to find a gentle way to explain that the daily nagging about homework and grades both perpetuates Marianna's dependence on her mother's interventions and teaches her that external rewards are far more important than the effort Marianna invests in her education. Marianna is so concerned with pleasing her parents that the love she used to feel for learning has been crowded out by her craving for validation.

This mother's hovering comes from a place of love, that's clear. She wants the world for her children, and yet the very things she's doing to encourage the sort of achievement she feels will help them secure happiness and honours may be undermining their future success.

Marianna is very smart, and her mother reminds her of that on a daily basis. However, Marianna does not get praised for the diligence and effort she puts in to sticking with a hard maths problem or a convoluted scientific inquiry. If that answer at the end of the page is wrong, or if she arrives at a dead end in her research, she has failed, no matter what she has learned from her struggle. And yet contrary to what she may believe, in these more difficult situations she *is* learning. She learns to be creative in her problem-solving. She learns diligence. She learns self-control and perseverance. But because she is scared to death of failing, she has started to take fewer intellectual risks. She knows that if she tries something challenging or new, and fails, that failure will be hard evidence that she's not as smart as everyone keeps telling her she is. Better to be safe. Is that

> I look at this mother with concern on her face, her eager pencil poised to write down my words of wisdom, and struggle to find a gentle way to explain...

what we want? Kids who get straight A's but hate learning? Kids who achieve academically but are too afraid to take leaps into the unknown?

Marianna's mother has been extremely successful in school and business and she knows the value of that hard work in her own life. Her mother allowed her to fail and play and learn for the sake of learning, but now that she's parenting her own child, she's lost sight of the value of struggle. She is too worried about Marianna's future achievements to allow her to work through the obstacles in her path. She wants to give Marianna everything and yet she forgets that the very best experiences of her own childhood likely arose from facing challenge, from the moments she lost herself in the trying, and when she failed, trying again to accomplish something all on her own, simply for the adventure and pleasure inherent in taking on something new.

I know this mom because she's just like me, and telling her the truth is hard both because I'm afraid she'll get defensive and angry, and because it means I have to admit to all the same mistakes she's made. Maybe it's time to share some truths as I figure out where I went astray so that together we can help our kids rediscover their intellectual bravery, their enthusiasm for learning and the resilience they need in order to grow into independent, competent adults. With a little luck, they will look back on their childhood and thank us; not just for our unwavering love, but for our willingness to put their long-term developmental and emotional needs before their short-term happiness. To let their lives be just a little bit harder today so they will know how to face hardship tomorrow.

Intrinsic motivation: the holy grail of parenting

The less we push our kids toward educational success, the more they will learn. The less we use external, or extrinsic, rewards, the more our children will engage in their education for the sake and love of learning.

All kids begin life motivated by a desire to explore, create and build. When babies take their first steps, it is because they are driven to discover and master their environment. If there's any trick to parenting, it is to keep our children from losing that internal drive. Unfortunately, today's parents and teachers increasingly rely on the same sort of reward system used to train monkeys and seals. It works well at the circus, but bananas and herring – or iPads and pizza – do not work for humans. Rewards may get results in the short term, but when it comes to encouraging long-term drive and enthusiasm for learning, rewards are terrible motivators.

When I read about the latest thinking on rewards, first in Daniel Pink's *Drive*, and later in the original research of psychologists Harry Harlow and Edward Deci, I was thrown. Nearly everything I do in my classroom and in my home revolves around external rewards, but Harlow's research into what motivates monkeys had me doubting my practices.

In 1949, Harlow became curious about what motivates primates (and, by extension, humans). He gave eight monkeys, each in its own cage, a latch attached to a piece of wood, and waited to see what they would do with it. He didn't have to wait long; the monkeys loved playing with the latches, and fiddled with them over and over again until they opened up. The monkeys were opening the locks just for the fun of the activity, or, in Harlow's words, "the performance of the task provided intrinsic reward." That's all the monkeys needed to spur them on.

Once Harlow realised the power of intrinsic motivation, he was curious about whether an "extrinsic reward" such as a raisin would improve their performance.

In the second phase of his experiment, Harlow gave half of the monkeys a raisin as a reward for opening the locks. The monkeys were quite good at opening the locks, so surely, given a reward, they would open them even faster, right?

Nope. The monkeys who received raisins actually opened the locks more slowly, and with less frequency, than they did when no reward was offered. Something about the extrinsic reward interfered with their intrinsic motivation and threw them off their game (or latch, in this case).

The human analogy is simple: when a kid is fascinated by a task, he will be much more likely to persevere, even when he falters, even when the task gets more challenging, and yes, even when he fails to master the task the first time around. Think back to the explorations of your newly mobile baby, crawling around the living room floor, pulling the cat's tail, and clearing the books off the bottom shelf of the bookcase. My sons drove me crazy, dropping spoons down into the heating vent in the living room and repeatedly attempting to climb the stairs on their own. That same drive that allows kids to learn the name of every player in the premier league or the scientific name and genus of every dinosaur that lived during the Cretaceous period fuels their learning early on in school. As kids get older, our goal should be to preserve this natural curiosity and thirst for discovery at all costs. Unfortunately, the methods we use to motivate our children, such as rewards, are in direct conflict with what keeps kids engaged and interested. Put simply, if you'd like your child to lose interest and stop doing his schoolwork, pay him for good grades.

Once, many years ago, I had a student who was, according to her father, "a bad speller". No matter what the student did, she failed her weekly list of ten spelling words. Her grades hovered around a B, but that pesky spelling grade kept pulling her down into B-minus territory. Her year-end grade was, in fact, a B-minus, and her parents were livid. Not with her, but with me. They demanded an immediate parent-teacher meeting and asked some key school administrators to attend as well. They made it very clear in the meeting that their daughter wasn't "a B-minus student". The mother explained that, despite all the support their daughter was being given, she was intrinsically a bad speller and shouldn't be penalised for that. The meeting took about an hour and a half, and for much of that time, I was berated by the parents for being an ineffectual teacher and warned that my actions had lowered their daughter's self-esteem to the point that she cried every Thursday night before her Friday spelling quiz.

I used all of my best parent-teacher skills: I listened, kept my body language relaxed, and empathised with their frustration. I also made them a promise. I promised them that if they would allow the B-minus to stand, and encourage and value their daughter's effort rather than her grades, they might find that this B-minus "crisis" would be one of the best things that ever happened to her. They were not exactly mollified. They left that meeting extremely angry that I would not change her grade, and I left feeling frustrated and wary of the fact that I would be teaching their daughter again the following year. I hoped that some of what I offered up as advice might sink in, and that one day, we could all laugh over the B-minus.

That next September, their daughter returned to school with renewed vigour and a commitment to her education. Whatever had gone down at their house over the summer, *something* was working. She studied hard for her spelling quizzes and hit the ground running with a 10/10 on her first quiz. The good grades continued, and about a month into the year, I congratulated her on another perfect score. I motioned to the recycling bin and raised my eyebrows in a silent "Would you like the quiz back, or should I recycle it?" She walked up to my desk to retrieve the quiz and told me, "I have to have the sheet or I won't get my ten dollars."

Ah. She'd been getting paid a cool ten bucks for each perfect score. I was mildly irked, but then again, I thought, what was the harm? Her parents had the money to spend on the weekly, ten-point quizzes, she had some spending money in her pocket, and her past as "a bad speller" seemed to have faded into an unpleasant memory. Besides, she was happy. The arrangement seemed to benefit everyone, and it even worked. For a while. Some time after the holidays, her spelling grades fell again. I asked, and yes, her parents were still offering ten dollars for every perfect score. It was a busy year for her, she said, but she would bring her scores back up to where they were before, she promised. Except those scores never did come back up, and she ended the year, spelling-wise, about where she'd been the year before.

So what went wrong? If the ten dollars were incentive enough for that first month or two, why did the reward stop working? There are a couple of issues at play here. First, rewards don't work, because humans perceive them as attempts to control behaviour, which undermines intrinsic motivation. Second, human beings are more likely to stick with tasks that arise out of their own free will and personal choice. Given the choice between sticking with an "I have to" task or doing something else, most people would choose anything that is the product of self-determination.

Psychologist Edward Deci, author of *Why We Do What We Do: Understanding Self-Motivation*, provided the human extension to Harry Harlow's work on intrinsic motivation in monkeys. Deci sought to find out why younger children are so clearly fuelled by curiosity and a desire to understand their world, and why that internal drive is often lost in older children. "I had the fleeting – and surely blasphemous – thought that maybe all the rewards, rules and regimentation that were so widely used to motivate schoolchildren were themselves the villains, promoting not an excited state of learning but a sad state of apathy."

To expose these villains and prove his theory, Deci needed an inherently interesting task and some subjects. He discovered the Parker Brothers game Soma, "The World's Finest Cube Puzzle Game", and was immediately hooked on the challenge and feeling of accomplishment he discovered when he solved the puzzles. According to Deci, the Soma challenges were quite addictive, and he found himself solving puzzles in his head, even after he'd put them down. He then invited student test subjects into his lab to solve the puzzles. Some of the students received a dollar for every puzzle solved, and some received nothing and had to rely on their own feelings of satisfaction. After the subjects had solved a few puzzles, Deci would leave the room for eight minutes to complete an administrative task, and the subjects were left alone in the lab with the puzzles and an array of magazines. During those eight minutes, the subjects were secretly watched by the researcher to see how they spent their free time. The students who were being paid to complete the puzzles were much less likely to play with them, while the subjects who were not being paid continued to play, just for their personal enjoyment of the activity. In Deci's view, money does not motivate, so much as it controls, and that control disrupts our sense of intrinsic motivation.

After a few more studies in this vein, he concluded that just about anything humans perceive as controlling is detrimental to long-term motivation, and therefore, learning. Want to hover over your kids to make sure they dot their i's and cross the t's on their homework? Detrimental. Feel the need to impose some of your goals on their learning?

Detrimental. Itching to impose a deadline for your son's rough draft on that science project? Detrimental.

Don't believe me? Try this simple exercise. Go into a young child's room and ask to play Lego with her. If you play according to her script, everything will go fine. However, if you start to impose your goals on the project or attempt to force new directions based on your wants or needs, the fun will end, and quickly. Your child will either lose interest or get angry, but either way, your child will be done with that project. The quickest way to kill off your child's interest in a game, topic, or experiment is to impose your will on her learning.

So what is a parent to do to if we can't bribe, supervise, or impose goals or deadlines? Believe it or not, the answer, no matter how counterintuitive it might feel, is to back off. Allow kids to have the control and autonomy they crave even if it means struggling with the task or situation at hand. In an experiment that built on his initial results in the Soma puzzle research trial, Deci offered half of his test subjects a choice of puzzles, and predictably, the half who were given a choice spent more time playing with the puzzles and reported having more fun than the subjects not given any choice. As soon as your child is capable of working on his own, and maybe even a little bit before he is completely independent, give him choices. This is a well-known and wonderful strategy for toddlers, who are stuck in a developmental stage in which they have very little control over their world, and yet their need for autonomy is high. Offering limited choices to toddlers – *do you want to wear the blue or the red sneakers* – gives the impression of control without allowing so much control that anarchy and chaos result.

Give school-aged children control and autonomy over

where, when and how they complete their schoolwork and let them make choices about the other important aspects of their lives such as friends, chores and sports – subjects we'll address in later chapters. Establish a few, basic non-negotiable expectations, such as "Homework has to be done on time," or "Curfew is at ten and I expect you to be here or call if something comes up." After those expectations are made clear, older children should be allowed the autonomy to figure out for themselves the precise manner and strategy they will use in order to fulfil these expectations. As long as your expectation is that homework will be done properly and on time, the question of where, when and how they complete it should be up to them.

Don't worry; this does not mean teachers and parents have no say in our children's learning. It just means that we have to abandon our current strategy and get creative. I'm not going to lie: putting this knowledge into practice in my teaching was a challenge. I love standing at the front of a classroom, dictating the whens, wheres and hows to my students, assigning my carefully thought out lessons, grading their work when students hand it in on the due date. I had been teaching this way for ten years, but given Deci's research, I was moved to shake my teaching up a little bit and see what happened. I experimented with project-based learning, in which students create real-world problems or questions and then figure out how to find answers themselves. Students define the scope, goals and steps in the project, and therefore feel a real sense of ownership over the learning. My first attempts at handing the educational reins over to my students were encouraging, and I used Deci's work as a blueprint for my lessons. The more I pulled back and allowed my students to come up with the details of their own projects, assessments and learning, the more invested they became in those projects. I had to up-end my thinking in the classroom, and then, as I saw my students engage more enthusiastically in their learning at school, I realised I had to try these new strategies out at home with my own kids.

I took the guidelines I'd gleaned from Deci, set aside time alone to talk with my husband, and laid it all out for him: if intrinsic motivation happens when kids feel autonomous, competent and connected to the people and world around them, those three needs must inform our parenting.

Autonomy: in which kids find out that self-reliance feels great

Autonomy and independence are similar beasts, but their roots reveal a key difference. Independence is the linguistic opposite of dependence, but autonomy is something more. It comes from the Greek *auto*, which means "self," and *nomos*, which means "custom" or "law," so to be autonomous, a child has to have internalised a system of rules for living independently. In order to help foster the formation of this self-rule, parents have to help kids come up with a system of guiding principles so they will be able to problem-solve and think creatively while remaining rooted in tried-and-tested principles of behaviour. When parents are over-controlling, kids tend not to think about why and how they act in the world. Their choice is to respond to our rules or not. When they are given more control over their worlds, they are more likely to make solid, rule-based decisions. It's a win-win situation for parents, really, because autonomy begets autonomy. As kids realise they have control over their worlds, they want more control over their lives and become more responsible.

While the research on intrinsic motivation shows that attempting to exert control over kids undermines their sense of autonomy, this does *not* mean that we should not make demands of our children. Just the opposite. Children of all ages need limits and guidance from parents and teachers. Without limits, chaos ensues, and a chaotic classroom or household does not foster learning. I've spent a lot of time in other teachers' classrooms, and when those teachers have poor classroom management skills and fail to set expectations for behaviour, their students tend to be confused and are less likely to pay attention. In classrooms where teachers establish respect for the educational process and make their expectations clear, students are able to relax and focus on learning.

Applying pressure in the form of control is the single most damaging thing parents and teachers can do to their children's learning. Whether in the form of threats, bribes, deals, surveillance, imposed goals, evaluations, or even rewards and praise, control is the enemy of autonomy. We parents are all guilty. Full disclosure: there's a chore chart on my refrigerator, and on top of that same refrigerator is my son's favourite toy, a stuffed creature named Stinky, currently being held hostage until his room is clean and Finn is nearly apoplectic. I had a moment of weakness fuelled by frustration and accidentally reached into my old bag of parenting tricks when I made the decision to take Stinky away, and once I did it, I had to follow through. Parenting is hard, and even those of us who know what works in the abstract fall victim to old habits. That said, the research of Deci and others is clear: any strategy that undermines autonomy is probably not going to work if long-term learning is the goal.

Another drawback to offering rewards as incentive is that this strategy inhibits creativity and risk-taking. When rewards are at stake, emphasis is on the end result, so what's the point of creativity? If my students know they will receive an iPod for an A, they will take the safest route to that A, because they don't want to risk the iPod reward. The student who is motivated by the process of problem-solving and intellectual exploration learns for the sake of learning, and if the A comes, or the iPod falls into her lap, great. This is why intermittent rewards can work, while routine, expected rewards do not. The thrill and surprise of a reward when you least expect it can jumpstart motivation, but only when it's not part of a routine practice.

Weaning children off a reward system doesn't happen in a day, particularly if it has become your default parenting strategy. Remember, trained seals don't balance balls on their noses when there are no fish on offer. The behaviours you have been eliciting with rewards may well stop as soon as the rewards disappear. This will likely be frustrating to both you and your child in the short term, so it might be worth talking to your older children about why you are ending the system they have come to expect. You are the model for your child's behaviour and attitude toward failure. Children need to see examples of adults admitting to their mistakes, learning how to be better parents and people, and adopting new strategies when a previous one has failed. Make sure they know that you truly believe learning springs from failure, and encourage them to view failure in the same light. Anne Sobel, a lecturer in cinematography and directing at Northwestern University in Qatar, has fought back against her students' inclination to play it safe, by incorporating risk-taking and failure into her grading.

"I tell students that if they attempt a challenging project, I will take that into consideration when I grade, even if the film falls short of their vision."

In my own teaching, I make it a practice to model a constructive and adaptive reaction to failure. I admit to my mistakes and am honest about the moments my teaching strategies have failed my students. Those admissions have led to some of the most productive and cooperative moments in my classroom. Modelling is a powerful educational strategy – far more powerful than the offer of an iPod or ten bucks.

It was easier for me to admit to my mistakes in the classroom than in my own home. In the middle of an argument with my teenager, or when I'd grabbed the reins on some household task that had spiralled out of control, I could feel my heels digging in, even when I knew I'd screwed up. I had to push my pride aside and admit to my mistakes, and show my kids that I have the courage to fail, face it, take the lessons to heart, and move on.

When my husband and I stopped dangling rewards in front of our kids, we decided to try using something I had been using for ages at school: goals. My former school uses an advisory system, and teachers meet weekly with students to help them set goals regarding everything from school to social issues to handwriting. I think goals work well for students because they are rewards that remain squarely under the kid's control. Sometimes, when I feel my advisees could use a sense of renewal or a clean slate, we talk about starting from scratch with new goals for the term. For example, one of my advisees set goals to get over her shyness, and we devised plans for talking to teachers and asking other adults for help. She made huge strides, because it was *her* goal, to be completed according to *her* parameters, and if she failed, so what? She was accountable to no one but herself for those failures. Self-imposed goals are about the safest place there is for a kid to fail. If kids make up their own goals, on their own timeline, according to their criteria, then failure is not a crushing defeat. Goals can be amended, changed according to circumstances, and even postponed to maybe next week. For kids who are particularly afraid and anxious about failing, goals offer a private proving ground, a safe way to take risks, fail and try again.

If we really want our kids to invest in long-term goals, those goals have to be their goals, not ours. A friend of mine figured this out recently when her son pleaded to stop taking piano lessons. She was finally swayed when he told her, "Mom, I think playing piano is your goal, not mine." This can be hard to keep in mind, particularly when a student is having problems, but for a goal to work, the child has to own it.

Teenagers may resist the practice of goal-setting, particularly if you have been a controlling parent until now (I believe my older son mocked the entire idea the first couple of times I brought it up). However, once they realise that you have turned over a new leaf and want to help them achieve *their* goals, their trust in your motives will return. And remember, this goal-setting does not have to be conducted like a business meeting. The best discussions are relaxed, calm and casual. My favourite conversations take place in the car, on walks, and in all those moments that pop up when you least expect them. Teenagers are not always ready to listen or talk, and sometimes you simply have to be ready to meet them where they are and when their minds and spirits are willing.

Be supportive of their goals. Some goals are going to

seem trivial, but if they are important enough for your child to verbalise, they are important enough for your respect and support. Deci calls this strategy "autonomy-supportive," but I call it smart parenting.

Competence: confidence born out of experience

You can prop your child's confidence up with lavish praise, but you cannot create competence through praise alone. Competence requires both ability *and* experience, and confidence alone can lead to disaster. Recent studies have shown that, while kids need to engage in free play that includes risk-taking, risky play is much more dangerous for kids who have never been allowed to engage in it than for kids who grow up knowing how to manage risk. Knowing how to manage risk through experience is real, hard-earned competence, and it makes them feel great about themselves.

When my neighbour's son was five, he was absolutely positive he could operate his father's power tools. As his father had not yet taught him to use any of those tools, this belief was built on confidence rather than competence. On one visit to his house, he led me over to his father's new wood splitter, an insanely dangerous and decidedly not kid-approved piece of machinery. He looked up at me with great hope (and a hand on the power key) and asked if I'd like to see him operate it. I declined his offer (and alerted his mother), as I knew his confidence was grounded in nothing more than his deep love of power tools. Now that he is nearly twelve, and his father has spent hours teaching him how to operate the machinery safely and effectively, he has become a competent carpenter, woodsman and handyman. That competence stems not just from a belief that he could work these tools but also from a place of real ability and hours of experience under his father's guidance.

Children who possess competence through experience will be safer in the world because they will not launch themselves headlong into risks they are unprepared to handle. A child who believes he's ready for the deep end of the pool because you praised his incredible talent as a swimmer when he flopped through his first two freestyle strokes is in much more danger of drowning than a child who has a realistic sense of his abilities. Be honest with your children. Praise them for their resilience and the efforts they make to recover from their mistakes. Above all, keep your eye on the prize: intrinsic motivation. Protecting kids from the frustration, anxiety and sadness they experience from failure in the short term keeps them from becoming resilient and from experiencing the growth mindset they deserve.

On one visit to his house, he led me over to his father's new wood splitter, an insanely dangerous and decidedly not kid-approved piece of machinery. He looked up at me with great hope (and a hand on the power key) and asked if I'd like to see him operate it...

Encourage competence in your child whenever possible. Watch a child making her own lunch, or listen to a teenager recount the moment he scored a goal in football. Competence and mastery are incredible motivators. Once children get a taste of success, particularly success born of their own efforts and persistence, it becomes addictive. This is the lovely thing about competence: it's a self-fulfilling prophecy.

I have seen what can happen when a child who has previously been bribed and cajoled suddenly discovers the joy of doing something for oneself. It's as if the sun has broken through the clouds. The best part of this moment is that once a kid masters a skill through his own self-directed efforts, he enters a positive feedback loop that keeps on giving. The buzz can last for years if it's nurtured. I've even seen this sense of competence overshadow and replace years of frustration and negative self-image.

The key is that competence must come out of a child's own efforts. Keep this in perspective as you begin to withdraw rewards (false praise, gifts, unnecessary adulation) and shift to a more autonomy-supportive system. The day your child comes home from school having finally understood a difficult concept, all radiant with pride and mastery, the magic of competency will become clear.

Connectedness

This last element of intrinsic motivation comes down to your child's relationships with you, with teachers, and with the world at large. Humans are social animals, and we need to know that our efforts mean something to other people and the world. The good news is that autonomy-supportive parenting tends to strengthen bonds between child and parent, whereas controlling practices weaken them. Again, this does not mean that parents who set strict limits are bad parents. One of the most effective mothers I've ever known is incredibly strict, but her children understand why she sets the limits she does. She reminds me a bit of Ma Ingalls, because above all else, she's reasonable and supportive of her children's autonomy and sense of competence. Consequently, her children, even her teenagers, admire and adore her, and feel connected to her to a degree that is rare these days.

In order to foster autonomy while strengthening that connection to your kids, you need to show them that you have confidence in their capacity to grow. Here's where the idea of "mindset" comes in. Stanford University psychology professor and *Mindset* author Carol Dweck divides people into one of two mindsets: fixed or growth. A person with a fixed mindset believes that intelligence, talent, or ability are innate, and remain the same throughout life, no matter what. A person with a growth mindset, however, believes that these qualities are simply a starting point, that more is always possible through effort and personal development. Those with growth mindsets are motivated to learn for learning's own sake because they believe that by pushing and stretching themselves they can do more and become more accomplished. They thrive on challenge and understand that failing and trying again is part of becoming smarter, better or faster. If they discover limitations in themselves, they search for ways to overcome these challenges. "The hallmark of successful individuals is that they love learning, they seek challenges, they value effort, and they persist in the face of obstacles," writes Dweck. To put this research in practical terms, kids with fixed mindsets will be far less likely to persevere when school gets challenging because they don't believe they can stretch beyond their perceived limitations. Kids with growth mindsets will push on even when they fail to understand something the first time around because they know it's a matter of exerting more effort until they succeed.

Sadly, over-parenting undermines so much of what contributes to a growth mindset. Over-parenting teaches kids that without our help, they will never be able to surmount challenges. When we save them from risk and failure, we communicate to our kids that we don't have faith in their ability to grow, improve and surmount challenges and we encourage a fixed mindset. And this, in turn, has an impact on their sense of connection, both to other people and to the world at large. Connectedness cannot forced, it grows out of trust, a trust on your part in your child's competence and on their part that you are not just seeking to exert control. We may feel "connected" to our children as we rescue them from difficulties but what we are communicating is our lack of confidence in them. A healthy connection is based on love and support rather than control and nurtures independence rather than dependence.

As I see it, this idea of connectedness goes beyond home to the classroom and the larger world outside because it makes what we do meaningful. *Why* are we learning about *Beowulf* or *Great Expectations*? What does the journey of the hero or Pip's coming of age have to do with *me*? As a teacher, I know that if I fail to build a connection between Roman culture and the roots of modern languages, Latin is for my student truly a dead language, and unlikely to inspire passion or drive in them.

So one of the most important things parents can do for their children is to show them that they are not alone in the world, that they matter in the big picture, and that their parents are there to support them as they find their place within it.

Desirable difficulties

While autonomy, competence and communication sound like great concepts in the abstract, allowing kids to make the mistakes and face the failures that flow from increased autonomy goes against our parenting instincts. It's hard to watch, and it's even harder to not jump in when we see our kids frustrated or upset. I get frequent emails from parents whose kids were frustrated by an assignment, or a quiz question wasn't phrased precisely the same way I'd phrased the material in class. We want life to be smooth sailing for our kids, but interesting research shows that smooth sailing isn't where real, deep learning happens. Small failures, when the stakes are relatively low and the potential for emotional and cognitive growth is high, are what psychologists Elizabeth and Robert Bjork call "desirable difficulties". Learning that comes with challenge is stored more effectively and more durably in the brain than learning that comes easily.

Learning occurs when we observe something – we hear, see, or otherwise experience information in some way – and our brains transform that perception into a representation our brains understand. This is called *encoding*. We perceive hundreds of experiences all day long, and yet we don't necessarily hold on to all of those perceptions in our long-term memory. In order to turn those ephemeral perceptions into long-term memory, we must *consolidate* them. Consolidation is the process of organising, sorting and ordering perceptions and experiences into something the brain can store away and pull up later. Finally, in order to really nail that memory down, we must tag it for retrieval later on. This final part of the process, retrieval, is vital to learning because it solidifies knowledge through the process of pulling the information back out of the brain in order to apply it to novel situations and contexts. This is why rote memorisation and regurgitation are ineffective teaching tools; they do not go far enough toward creating durable learning.

A popular buzzword in education today is mastery, and mastery demands retrieval. Students need to be able to recall information and apply it, connect it to other disciplines, demonstrate it for someone else, or otherwise render that information useful in their world. Teachers understand that you don't really know something until you can teach it to someone else, and this is because being able to teach information requires all three parts of the learning equation: encoding, consolidation, and retrieval.

But here's the catch. It turns out that the easier it is to retrieve information, the less durable the information is in your brain. So the harder you have to work to retrieve and apply knowledge in a novel way, the more durably that knowledge will be encoded.

That is why aversion to failure is a handicap. Errors are an integral part of learning. If kids are terrified of making mistakes, they will shy away from taking chances, to the detriment of their learning and personal growth.

In my work as a teacher, I talk to parents all the time who claim that their child simply can't abide failure, that it makes her anxious, upset and frustrated, which in turn makes parents anxious, upset and frustrated. They worry that, even if they adopt a rosy view of failure, their child is too afraid to fail. I tell them to watch their child undertake a task she loves, under her own motivation and control, and see just how afraid of failure that kid really is. A child who flips out over a challenging fractions equation during homework time is often the same child who will sit down to play Minecraft for three hours, gleefully overcoming repeated obstacles in order to construct the perfect lofty tower to house his stash of treasures and show off his architectural prowess. Our kids have not entirely lost their ability to face failure; they have simply misplaced it among their trophies and ribbons and award certificates.

Children can be taught how to rediscover their willingness to fail and tap into their intrinsic motivation, even when they have become reward junkies, slaves to praise, and dependent on our interventions at every turn. It's not going to be easy, especially in the transitional stage, but I promise, the ends will more than justify the challenge of the means.

3

LESS REALLY IS MORE: PARENTING FOR AUTONOMY AND COMPETENCE

When my husband and I started to transform our own parenting, we knew it would be a shock to the flawed system we'd been cultivating in our family for fifteen years. Rather than leave our kids to wonder whether their parents had completely lost the plot, we sat down one night with them and laid it all out – our parenting transgressions and our plans to reform. Yes, the teen rolled his eyes. Finn asked to be excused from the table about two minutes into the discussion. But when we admitted that we had been doing things all wrong, and that we believed that changing the way we parent would make them better, more independent, confident and *competent* people, I think I caught them listening. We told them that the more competent they became, the more we would let them do for themselves. The more we saw that they could handle difficult decisions, the more we would trust them to make those decisions independently.

There were some initial hiccups and setbacks, maybe even some pushback and tantrums, but once the kids figured out we had no plans to go back to our old ways of dependent parenting, they stepped up. My older son, who has always been fairly independent, started to take responsibility for everything in his life that I did not need to be a part of anymore. He started using the alarms on his calendar as a backup for his dodgy memory. He made checklists to help him remember the things he needs to do before the start of the school day. He organised his forms for high school and gave me what he needed me to read and sign. He took control of ordering his back-to-school supplies, packed for two weeks of camp, and left notes for me on the counter when people called. My younger son, who is usually willing and eager to let me do everything for him (recall our adventures in shoelace-tying), suddenly took charge of his morning tasks without being asked and even made a checklist after forgetting his towel one day at our local pool. He cleaned his room, organised his desk, and figured out where and when he planned to complete his homework every night. Best of all, he saw that my older son could do the laundry and asked to be taught how to use the washer and dryer, too.

Two weeks into our blissful honeymoon period, my younger son, Finnegan, suffered a minor blip in his journey toward autonomy. As the door slammed closed on the last kid heading for the school bus, I noticed his maths and spelling homework lying on the living room coffee table. I looked out the window at the bus stop, and there he was, oblivious to his oversight, twirling his hands in the air while explaining some detail of an imaginary world to his friend Pearce. I looked back down at the homework. And back out the window. And back to the homework.

And then I did my best to get on with my day, knowing that I was scheduled to stop by the school later, and it would be so easy to deliver Finn's homework to his classroom, maybe even surreptitiously slide it into his locker or backpack. He'd done such a good job on it, too, so conscientiously completing it in his neatest handwriting, effort now wasted. I picked it up off the table, looked at the neat letters and numbers, and put it down again.

Flummoxed, I turned to Facebook and posted,

> For those of you who think this whole letting my kids mess up thing is easy, know this. One of my sons left his homework assignment on the living room table, completed in a timely and neat fashion. I have to go to his school anyway to drop something off. Leaving that homework on the table, knowing it will cost him his recess today, is KILLING ME. I've looked at it twenty times, even picked it up once. But there it is. And there it will stay, waiting for him to see when he gets home and realises what he could have done to make sure that homework made it into his backpack and his teacher's hands.

Facebook friends began responding immediately, many with their pledges of support and enthusiastic approval and lots of "Likes," but one friend posted her strong disapproval.

> Jessica I admire you greatly, as I hope you know, but I could not do this. I forget things every day. I have driven things to my husband's office that he has left on the kitchen counter. I think a certain level of distraction is inevitable in our lives, no matter how hard we try, and high school kids are the most overwhelmed by it. I would be

so happy that the homework was done, on time, neat and ready that unless I was unable to do so, I would take it to school. I would save my consequences for homework that was not done or was not done well.

I thought about her words for the rest of the morning. I had to admit that yes, I *would* go out of my way to deliver a friend's forgotten wallet, or my husband's forgotten power cord, so why would I treat my children any differently?

Because I'm not raising those other people. I treat my children differently because I have a greater responsibility to them than to make them happy and grateful for my love and support. In order to raise competent, capable adults, I have to love them enough to put their learning before my happiness.

This shift in the way I understood my role as a parent was the hardest part of our switch to a more autonomy-supportive parenting style; harder than watching my kids mess up, harder than knowing they were going to mess up before they did and not preventing those car crashes. I had to stop equating the act of doing things for my children – saving them from themselves, scoring a smile and a hug when I showed up at school with a dropped mitten or toy – with good parenting. It still feels good to do things for them, and I still do, all the time. But the things I do for them are different now, and my motivations are based on an evaluation of *their* needs, not mine. Before, I was doing the things they could do for themselves to feel good about my parenting. Now, when I choose to do things for my children, I know my actions come from a place of genuine love, and I think my kids sense that too.

When I push parents to give their kids autonomy, I don't mean to imply that parents should drop all parental oversight and walk away, hoping the kids will respond by stepping up to the plate with newfound independence and intrinsic motivation. Autonomy-supportive parenting is not negligent parenting, and it is not permissive parenting. Autonomy-supportive parents establish specific and clear expectations, make themselves physically and emotionally present and offer guidance when kids get frustrated or need redirection. And the best part is that all the negative stuff we do to get our children to do the things we want them to do – nagging, nitpicking, hovering, directing – stops. These parenting techniques are destructive to our relationships with our kids, anyway, so parenting without them is a more peaceful and enjoyable affair all around.

Autonomy-supportive parenting gives kids what they need. Children today are too often starved of responsibility in the family; and all the jockeying for power, and the mischief that arises when their hands are idle, stems from our failure to give them a clear way to contribute to the family's wellbeing. Kids thrive on our expectations and they flourish when given responsibilities of their own and the education they need to carry them out successfully. That said, a certain degree of parental involvement is crucial for children's learning and emotional wellbeing. For example, study after study shows that a strong family-school bond leads to better educational and emotional outcomes and when teachers are polled, they point to "involved parents" as one of the most important elements of school success. This is still true, despite headlines from flawed, myopic research studies that have claimed parental involvement is over-rated. Teachers love parents who show up for parents' evenings, who help out with class trips and offer their support when it is needed. There is a difference, however, between being involved in your child's learning and taking over. The line between over-parenting and autonomy-supportive parenting can be hazy, but there is a clear difference between the kind of parenting that results in dependent, unmotivated and unsuccessful children and the kind that produces resilient, driven, intrinsically motivated kids.

In order to draw a line, and clarify why it's so important to support autonomy rather than dependence, I have to return to the research for a minute. Psychologist Wendy Grolnick has done some fascinating work on the impact that autonomy-supportive versus controlling parenting has on children's motivation. In her lab, she videotaped mother-child pairs for three minutes and rated mothers' interactions with their child as controlling or autonomy-supportive. When Grolnick invited these mother-child pairs back to the lab for a second visit, the children were put in a room by themselves to work at a task independently and the results were "striking". Children who had previously been directed in their play by controlling mothers gave up when faced with frustration in their solitary play.

Stop for a moment and realise what this means. The kids who were being raised by controlling or directive parents could not complete tasks on their own, but the kids who were being raised by autonomy-supportive parents stuck with tasks, even when they got frustrated. Kids who can redirect and stay engaged in tasks, even when they find those tasks difficult, become less and less dependent on guidance in order to focus, study, organise, and otherwise run their own lives. These competent, more self-reliant kids enjoy their work more. Children who rely on their parents to direct them through tasks, however, continue to require guidance and direction, and as the complexity of the task escalates with age and maturity, the complexity and nature of the parental intervention usually escalates as well. These are the kids who need their parents to help them with homework into secondary school and beyond. These are the kids who can't manage their schedules and priorities as they approach adulthood.

Sure, the leap from a controlling parenting style to autonomy-supportive parenting is challenging, but changing any habit is a challenge at first. Keep your eye on that brass ring of the positive feedback loop: the more independent you allow your children to be, the more independent they will become.

Making the switch will require some investment of time and patience. If your child never learned to pack his own lunch, do the laundry, clean out the car after school, load or unload the dishwasher, or do any of the many tasks any kid should be able to do by the time she starts secondary school, there's going to be a steep learning curve. The tasks may not get done to your exact specifications the first time around and there may be pushback as your child balks at his new responsibilities, but the rewards come, and sooner than you may expect.

While our children tend to love us no matter what we do or how we parent, I would rather my children think of me as the sort of parent who guides rather than directs, supports rather than controls, the sort of parent who is more concerned with their competence and the strength of our connection than with the alignment of the dishes in the dishwasher or the fact that a stray white sock has been tossed in with the coloured load of laundry.

Autonomy-supportive parenting is not the same thing as permissive parenting, because discipline, respect and rules all have an important place in this approach. Children need rules and behavioural guidelines. Most of all, children need structure. Young children test the boundaries of their capabilities but find it reassuring and safe when adults provide limits on their explorations. Toddlers test limits in order to be reassured that nothing has changed and that their world – including their parents and the rules they impose – can be relied upon. They test, we reassure, they relax, and the cycle repeats ad nauseam until that toddler finally gets shipped off to Siberia or enters kindergarten.

I try not to mention this in front of my students, but tweens and teens present a variant on the toddler's cycle of testing. They test their curfew; we reassure them that it's still ten o'clock and they relax. They test our resolve regarding boy-girl sleepovers; we reassure them that no, we still don't allow it, and they relax. They test our standards for their behaviour; we reassure them that we still expect them to be kind and respectful toward us and they relax. And the cycle repeats ad nauseam until the teenager gets kicked out of the house or starts college.

Testing limits is a way of testing independence, and that's a good thing, even if it makes us want to stick a fork in our heads. It's exhausting, yes, but it's a necessary part of creating independent kids. One way to make this testing easier is to establish clear expectations for their behaviour, and more important, stick to those expectations and employ consequences when those expectations are not met. This limit-setting is a key element of autonomy-supportive parenting. Limits are structure. Limits give kids reassuring information about what to expect and how to act according to those expectations. Limits make kids feel safe and cared for.

Parents who establish high standards and subsequently enforce those high standards are not *necessarily* controlling. In fact, there is plenty of evidence to show that children react favourably to parents who hold children accountable for lapses in behaviour or failure to uphold expectations. However, when parents resort to controlling behaviour in their attempts to hold children to standards – that is, when they offer bribes, rewards, engage in excessive monitoring, or apply too much pressure – this corrodes a child's sense of autonomy and therefore his intrinsic motivation (and, as we have established, his success in school and life).

Creating new habits

Once I'd weaned myself off my need to save my kids, I had to help them learn how to be in charge of their own lives. We taught them how to use the appliances and complete all sorts of household tasks but we also had to teach them how to form new habits; how to remember all those responsibilities and make them a part of their daily life. In *The Power of Habit*, Charles Duhigg explains that habits come out of a basic feedback loop: a cue, the routine and the reward. As an example, he writes about his habit of eating a cookie every afternoon around three. The cue (hunger or boredom) triggers a habit (going to the cafeteria), and the reward for the routine is both the satisfied hunger and the relief from boredom. In order to create new habits, you have to create a new cue, establish a routine tied to that cue and find an appropriate reward for the routine to close the feedback loop.

As we've seen, rewards may be antithetical to creating long-term success, but they can be powerful motivators when it comes to mundane, repetitive tasks – particularly if they are self-assigned. I asked my sons to think about what they do when they get home from school. My younger son said that he likes to do homework immediately after school so he does not have to think about it and can play with his Lego or draw in peace, but more often than not he gets distracted and his homework gets forgotten and has to be done in a rush later in the evening. We agreed that his cue for getting down to it would be his after-school snack. He'd come home, *prepare his own snack* (emphasis his!), and start his homework. The most important habits we all vowed to adopt have to do with technology. We all agreed that part of the routine for homework would include shutting down phones, iPods and other devices that distract us from our work.

We all agreed that the cue that none of us can resist is the sound of an email or text arriving in our inbox. And that if we omitted these cues, we wouldn't even be tempted to engage in the routine of checking emails and could enjoy the reward of homework completed without distractions. I assumed we'd have to come up with elaborate reward ideas, but in the end, increased independence was the reward my children had been craving all along.

> We all agreed that the one cue none of us can resist is the sound of an email or text arriving in our inbox.

Change is never easy, particularly in the first days. It definitely does not feel good, and there were moments along the way when I was feeling like a really mean and terrible mother. Given some time and persistence, however, change happens, and it feels great. Your kids will still make a stink here and there when they don't want to do something that needs to be done, but that's realistic. They are children. Even Laura Ingalls protested about having to do her chores once in a while. But, once your kids have detoxed off rewards, and the over-parenting withdrawal symptoms have subsided, your kids might just change their habits because they can, and because they want to. Because it feels good to be of use, first in our family, and later, in the big, wide world.

Because I spent months fumbling about in the hazy, grey area between controlling and autonomy-supportive parenting, I came up with some guidelines to clarify the difference:

Controlling parents give lots of unsolicited advice and direction

That's not the right way to load the dishwasher. Always rinse the plates before putting them in and stack all the large plates on the left side. Don't leave the dishes in the sink and come back later. Do it this way. Do it now. Do it better.

We all have our own way of doing household chores so there's every possibility that your child may not load the dishwasher precisely as you'd like it done. Unsolicited advice and direction, commonly known as "helping" from the parent's perspective or "nagging" from the child's, interferes with her sense of autonomy, conveys a lack of faith in her competence, and, because it's irritating and upsetting to both of you, undermines your connection.

When the child who loaded those food-laden plates

into the dishwasher unloads the dishwasher, she will discover that crusty food on the plate, and you will have the opportunity then to explain how to prevent that happening in the future. Offer guidance when the child is stuck, and seize the big learning moments, but otherwise hold your tongue. The mistakes she makes and corrects on her own are learning moments. The mistakes you anticipate don't benefit anyone, save for you in that brief moment when it makes you feel better that the plates are stacked northsouth instead of east-west.

Controlling parents take over

I'll do it, you go play. We have to get to school, I'll just do it myself when I get home. No, not that way, just let me do it.

Sometimes it's just easier to take over, particularly if you are under a time crunch or exhausted. Remember, the goal is for children to learn how to do for themselves, not for the task to get done. Sometimes it's going to be more important to be a minute late, particularly when a child masters something he's been struggling with. Step back, breathe and remember what's really important.

Controlling parents offer extrinsic motivators in exchange for behaviours

You get one jelly bean for every toy you clean up. If you walk the dog every morning, I'll buy you new trainers. If you load and unload the dishwasher for an entire week without being asked, I will get you that computer game you've been asking for.

As long as you keep rewards to a minimum and space them out, it's fine to celebrate or acknowledge in some way a child's accomplishment on the way to a more autonomous self. But many basic household responsibilities, such as walking the dog or taking out the garbage, should be viewed as part of family maintenance, not as endeavours deserving of hoopla or a grand reward. Everyone should contribute to what needs to be done around the house, and rewarding these kinds of basic activities suggests that doing them is heroic as opposed to expected.

Controlling parents provide solutions or the correct answer before the child has had a chance to really struggle with a problem

But honey, you know five times four is twenty, you just did that down here. I'll just look that word up for you while you do the spelling list. Just give me that pencil and I'll show you. Not like that, like this.

Not all answers come immediately. Give children time and silence to think. Not only will it teach them to value quiet; it also shows them that you value the process of coming up with the answer as much as the answer itself.

Controlling parents don't let children make their own decisions

Do your maths first, and then your spelling. Do your homework here at the table where I can see you. You should play tennis rather than baseball this season.

Sometimes it's better to allow your child to experience

the ownership and rush of independence that comes from choosing one sport over another or one game over another and that ownership is often more important than the activity. Decision-making is a complex process that takes a lot of practice, so give your child that opportunity to try on her autonomy for size.

Autonomy-supportive parents guide children toward solutions

I know you know what five times three is, so what happens when you add another five? Why do you think the cold glass broke when you poured hot water into it? We need to go via the library tomorrow morning, so what time do you think we should leave for school?

Parenting is teaching, and teachers look for the teachable moments in just about everything we do. Find those moments and lead your child toward answers. Discoveries that children make of their own accord will always be retained for longer and understood more deeply than the answers you hand them out of impatience.

Autonomy-supportive parents allow for mistakes and help children understand the consequences of those mistakes

It's no big deal that you dropped that glass, I'll show you how to clean it all up, and you can remember to carry fewer next time. Pick out the lumps in the oatmeal, and I'll show you a way to stop that happening next time. The mop bucket spilled because it's too short to hold the weight of the mop handle; just clean up the mess and use the other bucket next time.

It can be so hard to keep our sense of humour and patience when there's shattered glass or dirty water all over the kitchen floor, but if we show our kids that mistakes are part of the process of learning, they will feel more positive about their abilities and better able to bounce back from mistakes in future attempts. If we teach them that messing up means the world will crumble around them, we only succeed in reinforcing their fear of failure.

Autonomy-supportive parents value the mistakes as much as the successes

I'm so proud of you for sticking with that worksheet even though it was hard for you. What could you have said to your brother that might have helped him understand you rather than throw his toy at you?

One way to teach our children that we value mistakes as an educational tool is to support and love them as much during the mistakes as we do during the successes. Find the lessons in the failures. Help them discover new ways to cope and rebound from their mistakes in order to do better next time. Empathise and love them when they have messed up, because that's when they need our support the most.

Autonomy-supportive parents acknowledge children's feelings of frustration and disappointment

I get mad, too, when I can't do something right the first time, but I keep trying until I figure it out. Remember yesterday, when I did not get that job I wanted? That was really disappointing, but I know I'll figure something else out. I can imagine how frustrating this maths must be for you, but won't it feel great when you know how to do it?

Let your child know that you understand that algebra is hard sometimes and it must have felt terrible when Kayla refused to sit with her at lunch. We all need to feel heard and understood, and this is when connection happens. Show your child that you empathise with her feelings, and subsequent problem-solving will be much easier to hear.

Autonomy-supportive parents give feedback

Is your cardigan buttoned-up properly – something looks funny? If you forgot to carry the two in that other problem, maybe you made the same mistake on this problem?

Effective feedback supports effort and guides children toward seeing their own mistakes. Kids value supportive observations that encourage them to solve their own problems far more than specific directions because the solutions are their own, not yours.

As you make your way through the grey areas and begin to discern black from white, try to remember that the line between controlling and autonomy-supportive parenting is not always going to be easy to see. Sometimes it's going to be downright blurry, and some controlling behaviours, such as rewards and praise, can easily be mistaken for positive parenting.

You will make mistakes. We all do. But as long as we love our children, and make it clear to them that our love is not contingent on their performance, they will be fine. Research has shown that the worst kind of controlling parenting is the type that either withholds affection or makes it contingent on performance. This type of parenting hits kids where they are most vulnerable: their basic sense of safety and fear of abandonment. Even subtle withdrawal has a deleterious effect on children's sense of security, so be careful about how you interact with your children when you know you are disappointed in their performance. As long as we steer clear of this type of parenting, we can make a lot of other mistakes along the way.

Abandoning rewards and other forms of controlling parenting may seem counter-intuitive at first. But as parents get tired of parenting dependent children, and the positive effects of autonomy-supportive parenting catch on at home and in the classroom, all of this will begin to feel a lot less revolutionary and more like good old common sense.

———————————

As for my own dilemma over that forgotten homework, I fretted and puzzled over my decision. Why not just be nice, and give him a break, this one time? When it came time to head over to the school, and that homework whispered to me one last time, I realised why I could not, why bailing my children out and saving them from the consequences of their failures is different from doing my friends or husband a favour here and there. I went back inside the house to post my eureka moment to the Facebook thread:

As my discussions with Finn over the last couple of weeks

have been about packing away homework the night before so it does not get lost in the rush of morning, this is the perfect way to drive that point home. And Finn *does* know I have his back. I make sure he knows that every day, in every way, and yes, I forget and lose things, too (my keys, like 10 times a day) but those mistakes cause me to come up with strategies to help remember the next time. This homework is a specific response to a failure in his planning, and will pay dividends in the end.

When Finn came through the door at the end of the day, he was greeted by the smell of cookies baking. If I could not feed my need to feel like a good mother by delivering his homework and saving the day, I figured a batch of warm cookies might serve as a suitable alternative. All the love, none of the rescuing.

As he dumped his backpack on the floor and began to unpack his lunchbox, I asked him how his day went. I raised one eyebrow and pointed to the homework, still sitting on the coffee table. What did his teacher say, I asked, when he found out the homework was missing?

"It was okay. My teacher and I talked about how to remember my homework, and he said I could bring it tomorrow."

"That's it?" I asked. "No staying in from recess or giving up your free time?"

"Oh yeah. I had to do some extra maths practice during reading time, but I can just read for a bit longer tonight. And he made me promise to write a note in my homework book to help me remember to take my homework in tomorrow."

And he did just that. He wrote himself a note, and he remembered his homework the next day, and has done (almost) every day since. Facing the consequences of his failure taught him so many things that day. He learned to own up to his mistake, and talk to his teacher about solutions. He was encouraged to think about how to keep from making the same mistake again, and devised a system that worked for him. And, as we discovered when we sat down together after that night's homework was done, our cookies were warm, delicious and guilt-free.

4

ENCOURAGEMENT FROM THE SIDELINES: THE REAL CONNECTION BETWEEN PRAISE AND SELF-ESTEEM

One day, while picking raspberries with my friend Elena, we started talking about her daughter, Olivia. A year before, Olivia had suffered a severe head injury and lost her memory. At first, everyone thought it would return, but her life before the accident – her family, pets, friends, school – never came back. After about a month of waiting for her to remember the previous sixteen years of her life, Elena and her husband realised it was time to move on and make do with what Olivia had left. She was – and is – an otherwise capable and intelligent individual, albeit one without a past. I asked Elena how her parenting had changed over the past year, and reaching past me for a berry, she remarked,

I've totally changed the way I praise my kids. I used to just tell them how smart they were, how talented and amazing, but once Olivia lost her memory, praising her just for being smart and talented didn't feel right. She was working so hard to improve and to figure out who she was and who she was going to be that it made more sense to praise her for her effort, for sticking with this crappy, horrible deal she'd gotten. The kind of praise I was giving Olivia became the kind of praise I gave all of my kids, and it changed them, especially the younger ones. I can see a real difference in the way they think about themselves and their potential.

Praise is a tricky parenting tool, one that can lift a kid up or tear him down, depending on how it's used. It can give the kind of encouragement and support that makes kids want to risk failure and reach for greater challenges. Or it can destroy self-esteem. "You are a smart kid" is very different from "You worked so hard on that French homework." The first statement makes a judgment, and even if it seems like a positive and loving judgment, it has a negative effect on performance. "You are smart" judges and labels the person, not the product. If I tell my son that he's smart, I'm telling him that I value him for being smart, and he's going to be a lot less likely to try things that might damage his "smart" label, lest he fail, which, in his kid brain, could cause me to withdraw my love and approval. However, if I tell him that I am proud of him for the effort he's put in, I am reinforcing behaviour, not judging him.

As we have seen, children who are praised for effort are more likely to have a growth mindset, the understanding that intelligence and capability can be improved. In her book *Parenting Without Borders: Surprising Lessons Parents Around the World Can Teach Us*, Christine Gross-

Loh compares attitudes to effort in different parts of the world. At one extreme she finds that Americans are prone to a fixed mindset and are drawn to terms such as talented, gifted and prodigy, and therefore more likely to revere these inherent qualities. They are much more interested in the story of a child who can pick out a Bach concerto on a keyboard at the age of five than a violinist who has put in ten thousand hours of practice in order to rise to first seat in the orchestra. By contrast, in countries such as South Korea and Japan, potential is seen as a package deal, made up of innate traits and deliberate effort. Gross-Loh reports:

> When a teacher moves around the room, praising every kid, "Great job! You are so smart!" the students figure out pretty quickly that someone is being lied to.

> In Japan, there is less labeling. In school, students aren't separated according to ability. There is no "gifted" education, and most learning-disabled children are integrated into the regular classroom. Instead of dividing kids up, there is a pervasive belief – reinforced in school – that it's less about what you're born with than what you do. Up to a certain point *everyone* is capable of cultivating skills, even in art or music. So, while in America art and music are looked at as things for all kids to dabble in, but serious training or cultivation is reserved for kids who show talent, in East Asia there is a common belief

that anyone can and should be able to achieve a certain degree of mastery in a variety of areas, whether it be mathematics, art, music or physical education. It just takes effort.

The research on the harm we can do when we create fixed mindsets is best summed up in one of Carol Dweck's experiments. Dweck and her associates gave several hundred adolescent students ten test questions. After the test, half the students were praised with "Wow, you got [say] eight right. That's a really good score. *You must be smart at this.*" The other half heard, "Wow, you got [say] eight right. That's a really good score. *You must have worked really hard.*" The two groups did about the same on the test before they were praised, but after the praise was lavished, they began to look like two very different groups of kids. The half who received praise for their smartness adopted a fixed mindset. When given a choice between tasks, they rejected the more challenging option in favour of one they could more easily master, thereby keeping their "smart" or "talented" label intact.

Children look to their teachers and parents to help them understand their place in the world, and if we lavish praise for inherent qualities in an attempt to bolster their self-esteem, we do them a huge disservice. Not only are we instilling a fixed mindset; we are planting the seeds of distrust. When a teacher moves around the room, praising each kid, "Great job! You are so smart!" the students figure out pretty quickly that someone is being lied to. They know they can't *all* be geniuses, and they begin to doubt our honesty, or at the very least, our judgment.

And that matters. In the words of Lisa Endlich Heffernan, writer of the parenting blog *Grown and Flown*:

The single most important thing we have with our kids, beyond our enduring love, is our credibility. By telling kids that they are good at something when they are patently not, we ruin that credibility and do little for their self-esteem as the truth at some point will be revealed. When my kids do not have an aptitude for something, I don't shy away from telling them, but this means that any praise I do give them has that much more value. Our trustworthiness as parents should not be sacrificed on the flimsy altar of acclaim.

Kids who have been overpraised for their intelligence and talent are easy to spot in the classroom. They do the bare minimum required to get by; they never take up the gauntlet of challenging extra work and are reluctant to risk saying anything that might be wrong. These students are frustrating to teach because they won't stretch themselves or take any intellectual leaps of faith for fear of not living up to their parents' expectations and whatever label has been bestowed on them. The truth I try to impart to every single one of my students is this: it all gets hard eventually, even the stuff you have a talent for.

Imagine when a child who has been told that he has a talent for maths first sees a complex algebra formula in class and can't understand it. He thinks: "My parents tell me I am smart, but I can't be, not if I can't understand this right away, and I can't let them find out the truth." This is a terrible bind to put kids in and it drives them underground. They feel bad about themselves as they suffer through a crisis of confidence and identity, and reject help at the cost of the image they are desperate to keep intact for the sake of their parents' affection and approval.

The most striking part of Dweck's work on praise and mindsets lies in what comes after these growth or fixed mindsets take hold and begin to shape children's identities. After Dweck praised students either for effort or ability on a fairly easy test, they were then given a much harder test designed specifically to elicit some failure and frustration. The students who had been praised for their ability tended to give up, whereas those who had been praised for effort tried harder. These students didn't give up because they did not take the failure personally; they didn't think that their inability to give immediate correct answers meant that they weren't clever. Not only that, these young people actually said that they found the more challenging questions the most fun. That warms the cockles of my teaching heart!

> Kids who have been overpraised for their intelligence are easy to spot in the classroom. They are reluctant to risk saying anything that might be wrong.

While the students with the growth mindsets were having fun, the fixed-mindset students really struggled with the harder questions. Even when Dweck backed off and went back to setting easier questions, the fixed-mindset kids did poorly. They could not bounce back from defeat, and did worse on the easier questions than they had in round one. In a final, sinister, yet illuminating twist,

Dweck asked the subjects to write down their thoughts about the problems for future students and, while they were at it, write down their scores. Forty per cent of the kids who were praised for their ability lied about their scores. As Dweck wrote in her book *Mindset*, "we took ordinary children and made them into liars, simply by telling them they were smart."

In order to understand how praising kids the wrong way can turn them into liars, I turned to Professor James M. Lang, author of *Cheating Lessons: Learning from Academic Dishonesty*. He writes that we praise young people into a state of over-confidence and an over-inflated sense of their skill level, which can lead to all sorts of negative consequences, such as a tendency to understudy. The ability to judge one's own level of knowledge, skill, or thought process is called metacognition, and it's what allows kids to gauge whether or not they are prepared or knowledgeable on a topic.

Students with good metacognitive skills are more likely to achieve what Lang calls "self-efficacy," or a belief in their ability to succeed. Not confidence in their ability to succeed, not magical thinking based on parents' effusive praise, but a belief based on experience and repeated effort in a skill or task. Recent studies have shown that the very kids we hope to help the most with all this praise, kids with low self-esteem, are actually the worst off for our efforts, and suffer even lower self-esteem than if we'd just left them alone. Imagine what the less confident students could achieve if their parents and teachers started praising them for their hard work and diligence. That's the kind of esteem I'd like my students to have, the sort of self image that's been, hard-won, and deserved.

It's a real challenge to switch from a fixed to a growth mindset, and even harder to change the language that flies out of our mouths when our kids either do something well, or come up short. Don't worry if it takes a while to get the language right; we have become accustomed to the praise and encouragement we heap on kids for innate and effortless accomplishment. Even Carol Dweck admits to slipping up once in a while, praising her family for brilliance rather than efforts, but the point is to create new habits that have the potential to communicate an accurate representation of our children's abilities. Here are some ideas that can help reorient the way you praise your child, and may just help him adopt a growth mindset and strong sense of self-efficacy:

Praise for effort, not inherent qualities

Instead of "I love that drawing! You're so good at art!" Try "I love that drawing! Well done for taking such care with the shading." Kids who believe that ability grows with effort and diligence will be less distraught about failures, more likely to stick with tasks through those failures, and may even have more fun as they do so.

Adopt a growth mindset in your own life, even when it makes you uncomfortable

When your kids see you stretch yourself, even if you fail in the process, they will be more likely to stretch themselves. Better yet, let them see you continue to stretch yourself after you fail so they will understand that failing at a task does not mean that the person is a failure. You are your child's first and greatest role model, so show him that you are dedicated to the idea that success is tied to effort, not innate talent. Find the thing you believe you cannot do, and give it a shot. Failure and rejection are a part of the learning process, particularly when we move beyond our comfort zones, but it's amazing what can happen once we break out of our self-imposed limits.

Don't reinforce negative reactions to failure

We all react differently to failure, but some of those reactions are healthier than others and have the potential to teach us more. Denial, for example, tends to exacerbate and prolong failure. Be honest with your children. If your child has failed at something because she did not work hard enough, say so. Teach your child to see the realities of her shortcomings and failures and react accordingly. When we tell children how talented and gifted they are at a particular skill when all evidence points to the contrary, they know, and their faith in us is subsequently weakened.

Make sure your child knows his failures do not lessen your love or opinion of him

Your love and emotional connection buffer and soften the pain and embarrassment children may feel from failure. Further, knowing that you will be there to support, rather than judge or offer false praise, offers kids a secure and safe haven from the anxiety they experience in their lives.

Let your children feel disappointed by failure

Sit with the emotions and don't try to jump in and resolve the situation. After all, these are his failures, not yours, and it is unfair and counterproductive to try to make it all better for him. What you are teaching him through your patient silence and inaction on his behalf is that he has the inner strength to move on from failure.

Do not offer to rescue your child from the consequences of his mistakes

Your offer to rescue implies that you don't believe he has the ability to find a solution himself. Help him problem-solve and find lessons in the failure rather than viewing it as a devastating blow to his self image and confidence. Your goal should be to help him regain a sense of control over the experience of failing. The real learning happens when kids begin to understand how to pick through the wreckage, find the pieces that still work for them, and devise a strategy for future success.

Olivia eventually healed from her injuries, and despite having lost most of her knowledge base, she was able to return to high school, graduate with her classmates, and go to college. I can't be certain that the changes Elena made in her parenting had anything to do with Olivia's success, and a sample size of one is hardly statistically significant. I do know that when Elena began supporting Olivia's efforts rather than her intelligence, she increased the likelihood that Olivia would survive the many failures she encountered as she worked to regain a sense of normality. Better still, she gave Olivia a great lesson in how to be the sort of parent who will one day inspire a growth mindset in her own children.

Part II

Learning from Failure: Teaching Kids to Turn Mistakes into Success

5

OPPORTUNITIES FOR COMPETENCE

One afternoon, I walked into my English classroom and overheard a fourteen-year-old student complaining to her friends about how hungry she was. I asked her if she'd forgotten her lunch and she replied, "No, but I hate what my Mum packs for me." Rather than point out the obvious solution – that she should plan and pack her own food – I asked if she could think of any way to solve her unsatisfactory lunch situation.

"I could buy lunch...?" she offered, ending her sentence in an implied question mark, and looked for my reaction.

"Or..." I prompted.

"... or... I could... tell my mum what I like, so she can pack stuff I want to eat," she said more confidently, pleased that she had come up with such a brilliant plan.

"Or..." I repeated.

She was puzzled. What other option could there be? I turned to her classmate, who packed her own lunches.

"Elsie, what else could Kate do to make sure she gets exactly the kind of lunch she wants; one that she can't possibly complain about?"

Elsie turned pink.

"You could pack your own lunch. That's what I do. Sometimes I even pack lunch right after we eat dinner, because all of the food is already out, and then I don't have to do it in the morning when I'm in a rush."

It was Kate's turn to blush.

"Oh... yeah. I could do that."

And do that she did. In the first week or two, she even made a point to mention how much she was enjoying her lunch whenever I was in earshot. About a month later, on her birthday, she turned up in the door of my office bearing a large tray of cupcakes.

"It's my birthday. Would you like a cupcake? I made them myself." She was beaming, absolutely thrilled with this opportunity to make sure I knew how far she'd come in her culinary skills. I took one and watched her hand out the rest to her classmates, mentioning every thirty seconds or so that she'd made them herself. "Even the frosting!" she proclaimed.

Children want to feel capable, and we used to let them, before we took the onus of household duties away from them. Instead of teaching our children how to be responsible, reliable members of a family in which children contribute, we do everything for them. Worse, we don't expect competence from them, and when they do give household duties a shot, we swoop in and we fix.

We swoop in after our kids make their beds and smooth out the lumps and bumps. We swoop in after they fold the laundry and straighten the misfolded towels. I've actually taken the sponge out of my son's hands because he was making more of a mess of the milk he was supposed to be cleaning up. I have sent him out of the room and told him to "just go play" when he was not doing something as quickly, or as precisely, as I would have. I understand the impulse to want things done better, or faster, or straighter. But to what end? So much more than speed and perfection are sacrificed when we swoop in and fix.

What's more important – that the dishes are immaculate, or that your child develops a sense of purpose and pride because he's finally contributing in a real and valuable way to the family? That the bed is made without wrinkles, or that your child learns to make household tasks a part of his daily routine? All this swooping and fixing make for emotionally, intellectually and socially handicapped children, unsure of their direction or purpose without an adult on hand to guide them.

> Perfection is not what holds a family together; it is the bond forged through shared struggle that endures over the long haul.

It's important that my student plans and prepares her own lunch, not because she's spoiled or I want her to "toughen up," but because the failures she will experience when she screws up making that lunch are important. She needs to be disappointed in her own choices once in a while. It may sound petty but she needs to find out that when she packs yogurt under the ice pack rather than on top, it gets squished, and the entire lunch bag becomes a sticky, vanilla mess. She needs to know what it feels like to clean that sticky lunch bag and avoid the same mistake next time. She needs to discover all the small details, workarounds, and solutions we devise in order to avoid the million small disasters that plague ordinary, everyday obligations.

A friend recently had a car accident which left her un-scathed but chastened. She told me that in the midst of the crash, she realised that she needed to make lists of all the small details her family would need to know, if she was not there to take care of them. Her son needed to know that his soccer clothes had to go into the laundry on Sunday to be ready for Monday's practice. Her daughter needed to know which fabrics can go in the dryer and which cannot, and what happens when wool sweaters sneak into the dryer by mistake. The kids should know how to fix the toilet when it clogs, and reset the water pressure tank after a power outage and change a fuse, and use the lawn mower and the million other things she took care of on behalf of her family.

I pointed out that if she were to die in a car accident, the location of the reset lever on the water tank would be the least of her family's worries, but I understood her point. When we don't allow our children to participate in the business of running a household, they are quite helpless without us.

Protecting our kids from failure, from experiencing small disasters and learning how to cope with them, isn't doing them any favours. Some of our best parenting moments happen in the midst of disaster.

My friend and *New York Times* editor K. J. Dell'Antonia loves to tell the story of the day a friend's car veered off her icy driveway into a snowdrift. The adults were stressed and angered by the accident, but the six or seven kids on hand were thrilled and excited by the opportunity to pitch in and help get the car back on the road. They rallied together, fetching cat litter for traction and shovels. They devised all sorts of ramps and levers and pulley configurations in order to manoeuver the car out of the drift. K.J. still marvels at the optimism and enthusiasm that the kids brought to an otherwise frustrating situation. It was as if they were waiting for a crisis, an opportunity to prove just how ingenious and helpful they could be. They tried, and failed, at their many schemes to free the car, but they revelled in each new inspiration. K.J. speaks of that afternoon as one of her favourite memories of the winter and when I asked her son about the afternoon, he immediately broke into a smile as he launched into retelling the day's adventures.

When we exclude our kids from household disasters, we lose an easy opportunity to recover from these failures; household tasks can be daunting at first. We encourage them to be freeloaders and stick with the things they are good at: watching, being waited on, and making that face of perplexed impatience, hoping an adult will pass by and rescue them from their inability to solve problems. We teach our kids that they only need to worry about themselves, and risk pushing them over the line between ineffectual and incompetent right into lazy and narcissistic. Ineffectual and incompetent can be remedied with some patience but the re-education of a narcissist is a much bigger challenge.

In talking with teachers about what children are capable of doing around the house, it has become clear to me that teachers have much more faith in children's abilities than parents do. When I asked teachers for lists of skills that kids can do on their own, skills their parents don't believe they can handle, I received pages and pages of suggestions. One teacher, when faced with the question of what her kindergarten students could do if given enough time and patience, smiled and said, "everything". I have written my fair share of secondary school and university references and I can't begin to recount the number of times I've reviewed carefully written personal statements describing the students' commitment to service – time spent serving up dinners in homeless shelters, sorting donated clothing, building latrines in Costa Rica – yet I know for a fact that the young person in question has never done her own laundry. Many people spend huge amounts of energy and money on gap years and charity work and obsess about how these efforts will look on a university application, but a child's charitable education should begin at home, helping her own family, and sooner rather than later.

Just because your child has never done the laundry, or loaded the dishwasher, does not mean he is not capable of doing just that. Kids are creative and resourceful, and even tasks that seem unmanageable due to limits of heights or dexterity can be accomplished with the aid of a step ladder and simple directions. Those dishes that belong in the high cabinets above the counter? It took a half hour, but when my younger son was first assigned dishwasher duty at six or seven, he dragged a chair from the living room to reach the shelves. One by one, he put those plates away where they belonged. When I had asked him to "unload the dishwasher", I'd forgotten about the high shelves, but he'd figured a way around that obstacle himself. The look of pride he gave me when I said, "Wait – you did *all* of it? Even those plates?" was utterly gratifying. Failure has been a part of that process, of course. Since that first day, he has broken dishes in the process of learning how best to carry, stack and load them, but who cares? I'd trade ten broken plates for his smiles of competence and pride.

Children have been deprived of a sense of contribution and purpose for a couple of generations now, and it's time to give it back. Household participation is a first and, I'd argue, essential step toward building a purpose-driven and fulfilling life. When doctors examine causes of depression and suicidal ideation in adolescents, "lack of purpose" is mentioned over and over in the academic literature as a main factor. Purpose is what saves us all from despair when the details of life become overwhelming or boring, and it is what fuels the determination, resourcefulness and resolve that will see our children through to their goals.

There are a lot of reasons parents give for not granting their children the space and opportunity to find purpose, among them:

- It's faster if I do it myself.
- They will just do it wrong anyway.
- Kids should be kids while they can; they will work when they grow up.
- My house will look disgusting and people will judge me.
- My kids will look disgusting and people will judge me.

Enough. It's time to grant our kids the opportunity to contribute. Allow them the chance to step up, try, fail, and try again until they get it right.

As your child discovers his significance and purpose, it's important to keep in mind that he's going to fail. He's going to make a mess of things from time to time as he learns. His contribution to the household is not simply an item on a checklist you post on the refrigerator, but a process, an education. Get him to help you fold the laundry sometimes; if a shirt ends up all sleeves and no collar, not to worry. Let your daughter discover for herself that when she leaves the clothes in the dryer overnight, her favourite shirt becomes hopelessly wrinkled.. Eventually she'll become competent. Given enough time, and lots of opportunities, she may even figure out how to fold a fitted sheet.

As our children's first teachers, parents are in the best possible position to teach kids how to focus on goals and face everyday responsibilities and challenges with courage and a good attitude. If we are easily defeated, they will learn to become easily defeated. Children who view obstacles as overwhelming and insurmountable give up on their goals. Kids who have witnessed their parents' resolve and resourcefulness, and been allowed to develop great problem-solving skills, don't give up. They get down to the business of using pulleys, levers and all the other tools at their disposal to move obstacles out of their way and finish the job. Here's how the magic happens:

Great expectations and genuine accountability

Set clear expectations and hold your kids accountable when they don't meet those expectations. No bribes or rewards of cash payment – remember, those kinds of short-term incentives can be used to kickstart motivation, but don't work as a long-term strategy. Besides, the message should not be that one contributes to a family in exchange for money, but that one contributes because one is an integral part of a cooperative unit, a group of people who depend on each other for both labour and love.

Step away and hold your tongue

Once you've outlined your expectations for your children, explain that you will not be nagging them until they complete their responsibilities. If your daughter's job is to clean up her place after meals and rinse the dishes before putting them in the dishwasher, and she forgets, leave the dishes out. This is where the teachable moments happen. Explain to her that food dries over time, and will be much harder to clean off if left out.

This is going to require a lot of restraint on your part. Nagging and pestering is the fastest way to destroy motivation as well as destroy your connection and relationship with your child. Even if that dish sits on the table for two days, don't nag or hover, and absolutely no swooping or fixing, but be present and help problem-solve. Parenting coach and author Vicki Hoefle calls this method "duct-tape parenting" because, yes, sometimes keeping our mouths shut and holding ourselves back from interfering in these learning moments requires something strong. Keep the concept of autonomy-supportive parenting in mind and offer support, not control. Be there to help if he is not sure about a cycle setting on the washer, or if something goes horribly awry with the fabric softener, but find something absorbing to do while he goes about the work. No butting in, no prompting, and no correcting unless asked. Oh, and one last thing. If you go behind your child's back and redo the chore he has just finished to his satisfaction, even if it's after he's left the room, he'll notice. You will be telling him through your actions not only that he is incompetent, but that you will finish the job if he's careless. That is one lesson you don't want to him to learn, both for his sake and for yours.

Praise your children for the effort they put into the chores, particularly if they really had to problem-solve or had to stick with a task that was not going well. When I praised my son for putting those plates away in the high cupboards, I was not praising him for taking on the task, because he knew I expected that of him. Rather, I was praising him for the extra effort, determination and perseverance he showed when he hit a problem.

Ditch the lollipops

If your child has become addicted to the rewards you have been offering for helping out, you have a little extra work ahead of you to re-orient her thinking. Questions of "What do I get if I do that?" and "How much will you pay me?" must give way to a new motivation, and the transition can take time and patience. First, stop using rewards as your default strategy. If you must reward for household duties, try to put off the reward for as long as possible in order to disengage the reward from the actual task, or make the reward non-material. Keep in mind that little kids can only wait for a short period of time, but older kids can wait for much longer. The goal is to remove the task from the reward and shift their focus back toward internal motivators. As you move away from material rewards, talk about how rewarding it is to do a job well. Explain why you are not offering material rewards and why household participation is so important. Reward with praise the effort and patience your child had to exhibit in order to complete the task, even if it took many tries. *Especially* if it took many tries.

Once you have re-oriented your own thinking about your children's role in the household duties, and have shelved the rewards, here are some suggestions for what, and how, you can put your grand plans into action:

Preschool children

The key to successfully instilling a sense of responsibility and pride and helping children understand that they have a role to play in the family dynamic, is to start young. Even toddlers, with their diminutive hands and limited attention spans, can begin to explore their ability and competence in shared household responsibilities. When dealing with younger children be sure to make your expectations clear and age-appropriate. Katie Hurley, child and adolescent psycho-therapist and mother of two, gave me her perspective on how she empowers her young children with their household contributions: "My kids are still little and they might not make their beds the way I would, but the beds are made and they have pride of ownership – win/win. I see a lot of very controlling parents in my practice. Everything has to be perfect or punishments are the result. That's a mistake, and only ends up creating resentment and anxiety."

Communicate family participation as a privilege, or even a game, and toddlers can accomplish more than you might expect. They are capable of learning how to:

- Put their dirty clothes in a basket or hamper.
- Fold simple items of clothing or linens such as pillowcases or washcloths.
- Put their clothes away in drawers.
- Follow two or three step directions in order to complete tasks (get your toothbrush, put toothpaste on

it, brush your teeth).

- Throw rubbish and recycling away in the proper place.
- Feed the dog or cat.

Children aged between three and five can manage more complicated tasks. They are often big fans of counting and sorting, so give them jobs around the house that encourage them to practise these skills while instilling responsibility. Ask them to put five books on that shelf, or ask them to count out five oranges and place them in a bag at the store. Kids this age are perfectly able to:

- Make their bed.
- Sort and categorise items, such as utensils in a drawer, or socks in the laundry.
- Water plants.
- Learn to not freak out and cry about spills, but get a towel or sponge and clean them up by themselves.
- Prepare their own snacks.

Children as young as five can understand and accept the consequences of their actions (and inaction), but only if they experience those consequences. Forgot to put her favourite DVD away in its case after she watched it? The next time she wants to watch that movie, don't rush to help her look for it in the pile of loose DVDs. Refuses to put her clothes in the washing basket? She won't have her favourite pink jumper to wear to school.

These responsibilities and the lessons they carry are, of course, not really about DVDs or jumpers. They are about learning how to be responsible, to show initiative, and to follow through. They are about learning how to be the sort of person who will be able to manage the demands that life will place on them. If you constantly bail your child out, she learns a lot from that, too. She learns that self-sufficiency is not really necessary because you'll always pick up the pieces and that there's no real need to come up with any sort of system or plan for remembering her responsibilities in the future.

School-age kids

From the age of six children are able to develop reliable habits for completing household duties. It can be a real challenge to establish patterns during the unpredictable toddler and preschool years, but now is the time to make your child's jobs a daily event rather than an intermittent expectation. Habits are powerful motivators and tasks can't become habitual unless they are regular and expected, and, well, habitual. As we saw earlier, habits require three elements – a cue, a routine and a reward – and so in order to turn the occasional moment of "helping out" into a habit, it must be regular enough to become ingrained as a pattern.

Let's take loading the dishwasher as an example. Your child's cue to clean up after herself is the dirty dish in front of her at the end of a meal. The routine is the cleaning of that dish, and the reward is the sense of accomplishment and competence that comes from having completed her task. Again, this does not mean a material reward such as money or the promise of a toy or treat. The enduring reward is the sense of a job well done. Here's the best thing about habits: once they are formed, and your child completes her work as a matter of course rather than as a result of nagging, your household becomes a much more peaceful and harmonious place.

As I mentioned earlier, there are some exceptions to the no rewards rule. Rewards can be a fun and effective way to jumpstart motivation when it begins to flag. My favourite example comes from the book *All-of-a-Kind Family*, by Sydney Taylor. The book tells the story of an Orthodox Jewish family living on the Lower East Side of Manhattan in the early 1900s. The girls are responsible for household duties on a rotating basis and when the five daughters tire of the hated task of dusting the living room, their mother hides pennies in hard-to-find locations, locations that would only be revealed by a thorough job of dusting. Once enthusiasm has been restored for the task, and grumbling has been replaced with requests to be assigned to the task, she uses the game intermittently, just often enough to spark renewed motivation, but not frequently enough for it to become an expected reward. Once, in my own little twist on this lesson, I tucked a beloved missing toy into a pile of stuff I wanted my son to put away, and suggested that if he cleaned his room up, he might just find what he'd been looking for. My first impulse had been to shout to the heavens that Super Mum had found the toy, but that strategy would not have resulted in a cleaner room or the happiness and spontaneous discovery he experienced when he came across the toy himself.

Between the ages of six and eleven, children should grow more and more capable. They understand the concept of cause and effect and can predict that if the clothes don't go into the laundry basket, they won't get clean. If the dog does not get fed, she will be hungry. Capitalise on this understanding and help children see how being pro-active around the house can lead to positive effects. At this point, kids are able to be responsible for all sorts of household tasks, such as:

- Peeling and chopping vegetables (teach knife safety early, and always use a sharp knife, which is safer than a blunt one).
- Laundry – all of it, from sorting to putting it away.
- Replacing the toilet paper when it's gone.
- Setting and clearing the table.
- Outdoor work such as raking leaves, weeding.
- Vacuuming and mopping floors.
- Helping to plan and prepare grocery lists and meals.

Adolescents

I can't think of many household duties beyond the abilities of children aged twelve and up. The more competent teens I talked to for this book are responsible for:

- Household repairs, such as painting, replacing lightbulbs, and simple car maintenance.
- Grocery shopping.
- Planning and preparing more complicated meals.
- Caring for and teaching younger siblings.
- Taking the dog to the vet for his vaccinations.
- Chopping kindling and firewood.
- Clearing leaves out of the gutters.

Adolescent psychologist Jennifer Hartstein has this to say about the role household duties play in a teen's life: "Having to be responsible for things at home (i.e., chores, laundry, walking the dog, etc.) helps to teach teens what it means to take care of the important things in their lives. Ultimately, this will cause teens to have better self-esteem, feel more effective, be more productive, and be more motivated to continue this into their adult lives."

It's never too early, or too late, to teach children how to contribute and solve problems themselves. Despite all the protests to the contrary, kids want to play a useful role in their family's success. As parents, we have slowly, but systematically, deprived them of that role, and we owe them the patience and time it takes to give that purpose and responsibility back. Sure, this restoration of order will be a challenge, but it will also be worth it, both in the short and long term. The contribution of your children to the daily work of keeping a house running will not only be a boon to the family now, but will set them apart from their more coddled peers when they head off to university or land their first job. While their peers stand around helplessly, waiting to be told what to do and how to do it, your kids will know how to take charge and forge ahead, armed with the competence, experience and the skills they learned by your side, in your home. They have had opportunities to fail, to mess up and fix their errors, and won't be fazed by a misstep here and there as young adults. Better to understand now that perfection is not what holds a family together; the bond forged through shared struggle is what endures over the long haul.

6

FRIENDS: ACCOMPLICES TO FAILURE AND THE FORMATION OF IDENTITY

The dad running back and forth between the climbing frame and the sandpit meant well, we could tell, but watching him work himself up into a sweaty lather was exhausting, even from a distance. My friend and I watched from our bench in the shade, quietly nibbling our children's cheddar crackers.

One of his children, a girl of about six, was playing in the sandpit with my friend's daughter and two other girls. They were playing well together, but there was the usual jockeying for power going on between them, and they occasionally erupted in shouting as they fought over the coveted roles in their communal game. His other child, a toddler, was gleefully testing the limits of his strength and agility, repeatedly attempting to pursue a much older child up a slippery slide.

Both of his children were having a grand time in the

moments they were allowed to play on their own. The father, however, was nearly apoplectic with worry. He could not simultaneously supervise the details of both children's play, so he ran back and forth between the two, sometimes towing the toddler under his arm as the boy screamed in protest. Every time the girl's voice rose to a shout, or one of the other girls shouted at her, the father rushed in to sort out their issues, soothe, or bribe the girl with the promise of a snack if she would "just play nice". When one of the other girls spoke harshly to his daughter, his eyes swept the crowd, searching for back-up in the form of the other girls' parents. My friend wisely kept her mouth shut and averted her eyes when he looked in her direction. Meanwhile, his toddler seized on the opportunity of his father's momentary inattention to run back to the slide, which made the father so nervous that he abandoned the management of his daughter and ran back across the playground for round two.

I can only imagine how tiring and stressful the "play" session was for that dad. As for the kids, I can't imagine they enjoyed all his meddling. They seemed to have fun in fits and starts, but as soon as they gathered momentum and the play took on a life of its own, it was shut down due to noise or conflict. What that overwrought father did not understand was that with his extravagant over-parenting he was defeating the very purpose of their playtime.

Our children's social lives begin in infancy when they gaze up at our faces and mirror our smiles, or convey the soggy discomfort of a wet diaper with a wailing cry. Once those babies move beyond the close company of their parents and venture into relationships with other children, however, they begin a lifelong education in rules of social conduct and the vocabulary of the subtle cues human beings use to communicate with each other. Fluency in the language of human social interaction will determine the success of all their future relationships, and failure to develop fluency is a significant handicap in life.

Much of the foundation for this fluency is taught through free play with other children. In her book *The Nurture Assumption: Why Children Turn Out the Way They Do*, psychologist Judith Harris argues that parents matter much less in the development of our children's nature than we'd like to believe and that peers, not parents, shape much of our children's behaviour and experience of the world. Peers teach our children how to interact and negotiate with other people, and this education starts in the sandpit, where children learn to play co-operatively, respond to the needs of others, and construct their own imaginary worlds. Play is a vital part of human development for many reasons: board games teach logic and planning; spatial and construction skills are learnt by making forts and dens; football, netball, etc, teach teamwork as well as hand-eye co-ordination. But the most important lessons of play and friend time are interpersonal, and these lessons are best learned when uninterrupted and free of adult manipulations and machinations. Adults should give kids the space and freedom to learn this language and to work out the tough social moments for themselves, because those fights, tussles, silent treatments and breakups are, despite the tears and heartbreak they cause, invaluable opportunities for growth. The social conflicts of childhood are all part of our education in human relationships. Squabbles are opportunities to be valued, not emergencies to be managed. That father on the playground leapt in to intervene at the first sign of discord, and in doing so, short-circuited each one of those potential lessons. In the past, children used to play on their own, away from the eyes of parents and were allowed to work out these social dynamics free of parental interference. No longer.

When the troublesome, sand-throwing girl from the playground is removed from the squabble, she never learns to deal with her own anger, let alone the anger of her intended target. Worse, she never witnesses the rage and upset she caused. She needs to appreciate that she has failed at a social interaction and sit with those confusing, bad feelings. The target of the sand

By a whopping 40 per cent, peer play is significantly more predictive of academic success than standardised achievement tests.

attack, who does not appreciate having sand thrown in her face, will send a message about acceptable sandpit behaviour. In the end, the conflict will pass, and those two girls will likely heal their rift, and end up closer and wiser for the conflict. Sure, throwing sand is a failure to communicate effectively, but when adults intervene, children are deprived of the opportunity to learn from their peers. Children develop empathy by seeing and hearing other people's reactions and emotions, and when we don't allow our children to experience the full brunt of those uncomfortable moments, we deny them a glimpse into the consequences and impact of their actions on others. One missed lesson in the sandpit is no big deal, of course, but when that child who grows up under the wing of parents who continually rescue him from playground dust-ups moves on to the inevitable volatility of adolescent friendships, that child is becoming an adult with no clue about how to negotiate, placate, reason with and stand up to other adults.

Andrea Nair, a psychotherapist and parenting coach, explains this to me further:

> The cost of overprotecting is that the child does not develop the skills to fight back, speak up or get the hell out of the way. If a child is taught by their parent that an adult will swoop in and fight for them or save them from any form of challenging situation, that child will keep expecting that to happen and not look for solutions to help herself. That child will also not learn valuable communication skills that are necessary during the heat of emotional flooding during an argument.

If the emotional and social benefits of not swooping in to rescue kids from conflict are not sufficient to convince you, how about this: the ability to enjoy uninterrupted and unrestricted free play is also predictive of academic success.

In her book about American children, *A Nation of Wimps*, Hara Estroff Marano points out that social interactions cultivated during free play are "so important that social behaviour at recess in kindergarten predicts achievement at the end of first grade, as measured by class work and standardised tests of general knowledge, early reading, and maths concepts. By a whopping 40 per cent, peer play is significantly more predictive of academic success than standardised achievement tests. Free play, and the social interactions that it fosters, are undervalued in our children's social and emotional growth. It is a gross mistake to think that play is time unproductively spent." Sadly, many schools are so closely monitoring recess and managing children's social dynamics that kids don't have the opportunity or freedom to let recess and lunchtime dramas play out to their logical (and sometimes illogical) conclusions. This shortsighted and misguided move away from unsupervised free play means children have fewer opportunities to process the lessons they learn in school and are left with no outlet for the physical and emotional energy that builds up during the day. Later, when those recess-deprived children arrive home from school, they are no longer being kicked out of the house to fend for themselves until dinner; they are shuttled from organised activity to tutoring sessions and given precious little opportunity either to express their urge for unstructured play or indulge in skirmishes with their siblings.

As part of a study based at the Auckland University of Technology, eight elementary schools in New Zealand agreed to eliminate recess rules, relax supervision, and stop intervening in students' playtime. Consequently, those schools saw a reduction in bullying, fewer rule infractions, reduced need for adult supervision, and an improvement in attention and behaviour during class time. Grant Schofield, one of the researchers in the study, explains that backing off on adult supervision and interventions during free play allows kids "to think for themselves and sort [social interactions] out". When we interfere with our kids' social lives, they are deprived of yet another opportunity to learn how to sort out feelings, convictions and personal limits. The goals and lessons of children's social lives shift over time, but as they move from toddlerhood to adolescence, it's important to view friendships for what they are: opportunities for them to develop their own personalities, identities and choices and for us to gain perspective and feedback on who our children are becoming.

The push and pull of playdates

In toddlerhood, friends are usually plucked from whichever kids are closest in age or proximity. Unfortunately, parents are increasingly opting for digital companions over living, breathing ones, but I beg you, put the tablets, game consoles and televisions away, and arrange playdates with a variety of real, live children. Playdates don't just give you five minutes to breathe and enjoy your own social time with another parent; they give your child an opportunity to figure out what she likes and does not like in a companion. Give her that opportunity to learn about friendships by giving her space. Don't take charge of the playdate. Provide a safe environment and observe from afar. Unless injury is imminent, kids don't want or need you interfering in their play. Even pre-verbal children convey their wishes to playmates, and as they mature into their words, they will begin to voice their opinions, likes and dislikes. Feel free to instruct those squabbling toddlers to "use their words" but understand that they may not have the words to use. They are still developing the vocabulary they need in order to express their frustrations, and until they become more verbal, they may use their hands, teeth and feet to express displeasure.

Sibling rivalry and resolution

These rules of disengagement apply to sibling social dynamics as well, but it can be hard to remember when the screaming and squabbling become overwhelming. I've been known to intervene just to get the noise to stop. Siblings are our children's first friends, their first enemies and teachers, and it's really important to let them work out their issues with each other in their own time and on their own terms. I asked Julie Cole, writer, co-founder of Mabel's Labels and mother of six, how she handles the chaos and conflict.

> With six kids close in age, there's a lot of fun, a lot of love, and a lot of laughs. There's also a lot of bickering and getting into each other's business. I learned early on that I have better ways to spend my time than inserting myself into every disagreement. Short of putting them in a soundproof room, instead I laid out the ground rules for how to "fight fair" early on, and as such, they seem to be able to resolve most things on their own. To me, "fighting fair" means only bickering about the issue at hand, never bringing up something from the past to use against a sibling, and no name calling. This means after an argument, they are back playing together five minutes later without ever remembering they had a disagreement. "Fighting fair" means I can step away and let them solve their own problems, which prevents me from pulling my hair out and being a full-time mediator.

Playground politics

Primary-school-age children tend to pick friends based on shared interests rather than proximity, and their play gets much more complex. As independence grows and dexterity improves, they invent games and construct elaborate adventures with complex rules for the imagined worlds they conquer. This type of play is an important learning process because it's the beginning of their move toward independence and autonomy. No wonder superheroes are their idols; kids mimic the power, strength and sense of justice those heroes represent in order to feel powerful in their own lives. They are used to obeying our rules, but as they step away from the parental sphere of influence, they discover the power of autonomy and self-regulation. They explore their own ability to create and destroy entire realms, and negotiate those power struggles with the other children involved in the game. As the influence of their friends begins to gain in force, it's a good time to begin to talk to your child about peer pressure and what she might do if she is placed in a situation that makes her uncomfortable.

One mother told me about her concern that her eight-year-old daughter is making friends with kids who may not be a good influence, though she is also realising how much her daughter is learning from these relationships.

> My daughter has a burgeoning friendship with a girl in her class who isn't a "bad" kid, per se, but I'm troubled by what I hear about her. She lies, she is rather boy crazy, and she is rude. But she also seems to have a pretty horrific home life – which makes me feel really awful for her. I don't want to completely discourage the friendship because I do feel like some kids can "turn it around". Also, the friendship seems to be teaching my daughter compassion. She knows, for example, that the child not well off, and she has been begging me to buy the little girl things since they became friends – things that my daughter used to take for granted, but now realises her friend does not have.

Kids are not born knowing how to manage for themselves and their friendships; they learn this skill through years of trying, and failing, to navigate their lives and their relationships. When a child learns how to say no to an older kid who asks to play doctor behind the toolshed, he also creates the emotional groundwork for some day being confident enough to stand up to a bully or demand fair treatment from an adult.

Parents need to step back and allow minor playground squabbles to happen because these conflicts give children a chance to learn how to handle themselves in an increasingly powerful bully culture. We need to remember that if Johnny pushes another kid down on the pavement, but is not allowed to receive feedback from his peers because teachers or over-protective parents whisk him or his victim away before resolution can occur, Johnny does not receive the benefit of peer feedback. In the absence of peer feedback, empathy can't develop, and he will become the sort of person who can't understand how his actions impact his classmates and friends. All those adults who intervened in the necessary lessons of his playground days are to blame. Unfortunately, a few years later, when he realises no one wants to play with him and his teacher informs his parents that he has "issues with his social skills," Johnny's social and emotional problems will be much harder to remedy.

The good news is that given time, and some space from adult intervention, children learn these social skills on their own. If we allow them to mess up, anger other kids, fight, and make up, they will be much more likely to learn how to be a good friend, how to stand up for themselves, and how to say no to behaviours that make them uncomfortable.

Research shows that children are less upset by their parents' arguments when they witness the emotional healing that results from making up, so it makes sense that kids benefit from seeing fights with friends through to resolution. Given that conflict is less upsetting to children than lack of closure, when you jump in to resolve a sandpit argument or forcefully challenge the mean girl who has been ignoring your daughter, resolution is not being allowed to happen naturally in its own time and place. Unresolved conflict triggers anxiety for children and gets in the way of the healthy process of making up and healing rifts with friends, moments which cement long-term relationships that will endure through the next disagreement.

Friendships in the middle years

As children move to secondary school, the focus shifts from shared interests to social acceptance. Cliques and other exclusionary social situations can be extremely stressful at this age, so it will be important to make sure that your child continues to participate in sports, music and other extracurricular activities that bridge the divide between social groups. One mother from New Jersey talked to me about the influence her own parents had on her approach to these issues:

> My parents left me to decide on my own friendships, and this was a great thing. I sometimes got my feelings hurt because I wouldn't do what [my friends] were doing, so they ousted me from their clique. It made me tougher and gave me pause when choosing friends.

Rather than dictate whom your child can associate with, make your home a comfortable gathering place for your child's friends, and set the expectation that when your child is not in your house, he will let you know where he is. Understand that kids' social lives are constantly evolving, and do not attempt to intervene when you feel your child has been excluded. You can be sympathetic to your child's sadness but don't try to fix a situation that is, and should be, out of your control. It can be painful to see your own child fail to make friends, or fall out with class mates, but these are important trials your child will learn from.

As a teacher, I have seen far too many students arrive at secondary school still unsure of how to handle social situations, but nothing upsets a child's social maturation more than parents who fight their children's battles for them. When parents over-react to everyday social inter-actions and label it bullying, children never learn how to stand up for themselves and demand respect. Bullying is a real and terrifying fact of life in schools today, but in our attempts to halt bullying before it ramps up into dangerous territory, teachers and parents tend to overplay the normal social and emotional ups and downs of the adolescent social scene and inadvertently saddle their kids with a victim mentality.

In talking to teachers and school administrators, it is clear that they are aware of the impact bullying can have on kids, but they are also frustrated by the way some parents inadvertently feed the bullying dynamic. One high school teacher told me:

I recently taught a student who had been the target of a few of her classmates' ire because of a disagreement, and when the disagreements and behaviours rose to the level of bullying, the school bent over backwards to make sure this girl was protected and safe. However, the parents – and consequently the child – became so hyperalert and oversensitive to what they saw as bullying that the teachers were forced to become secret agents. The entire class orbited around that one child's needs, from classroom seating charts, to teacher supervision during the walk between classes. The mother sent daily emails to the teachers and administrators, quoting her daughter's reports of mean looks, whispers and perceived slights. Normal social interaction could not take place in that class, and consequently, social dynamics were a disaster. The class ceased to be a community, and even academic progress took a hit that year. Worse, that girl came to view all uncomfortable social interaction as bullying. I am so sad for this child. Her parents mean well, but by moderating and weighing in on the subtle nuance of every social encounter, they have destroyed their daughter's confidence and convinced her that she is a helpless victim.

No matter how nervous these new and different friends make you feel, it's vital that you stay out of your child's social choices, particularly in adolescence.

As adults we all have our own bullies to deal with: mean bosses, aggressive neighbours or jealous peers. How your child learns to deal with those sorts of people in their childhood, when failure means a day or two of hurt feelings or social exclusion, can make the difference between a thin skin and a strong sense of self. As children get older, and friends play a greater role in their development of identity, it can be tempting to step in when you sense the presence of a bad influence. But before you criticise your child's friends, know this: making, keeping and deciding when and how to part with friends is part of your child's education. Something about that most dubious of friends attracts your child, and she is simply trying to figure out what that attraction is all about. Maybe that girl who dresses all in black and paints her nails green and swears more often than you are comfortable with has talents or social skills your child is trying to learn. Maybe your child is simply feeling out the limits of what she's comfortable with in her own world. No matter how nervous these strange and different friends make you feel, it's vital that you stay out of your child's social choices, particularly in adolescence. It may seem like a simple matter of a bad friendship to you, but your child is practising empathy and learning how to get along with people who may not share the same background and goals; these are incredibly important social skills. As adolescents move into college, they will adjust more easily to wider, more diverse, and often challenging social situations. In the business world, the ability to read all kinds of people is a sought after skill. These people, called chameleons or "high self-monitors," are better at adapting themselves to new people and to new work environments, and better at bringing other people around to their way of thinking. In sales, chameleons are able to connect to people through subtle cues of mimicry, and outperform other salespeople. In business, those who can adapt their behaviour to diverse groups of people make the best negotiators.

So when your son comes home from school with a new group of kids who make you uncomfortable because they are simply different from anyone you have seen him social-ise with before, think of their alternative approach to life as an education. If your child plays with carbon copies of the same four kids every day for the rest of his life, he will nev-er develop empathy for difference, or an understanding of how to negotiate and reason with people who come from differing perspectives, worldviews and ethnicities. Consid-er your polite smile and lack of judgment as an investment in your child's education, and back off. Let him figure out for himself what he likes and does not like in other people.

Learning from adolescent social angst

By the time your children become teenagers, you will be glad you stayed out of their social lives, because they will have superior skills of negotiation and self-awareness. As tweens become teens, and perceived dangers can become real dangers, these are inevitably going to be occasions when you will wonder whether it's time to intervene. De-pending on whom you ask, this question will get many different answers, from "five minutes ago" to "never". I'm always going to err on the side of trusting my child in order to preserve autonomy but, out of curiosity, I asked a group of fifteen-year-olds to answer this question. Most of the kids felt it was perfectly reasonable for a parent to snoop if that parent had a *reason* to snoop. "If someone told you that your kid was doing something dangerous," clarified one boy. In talking to these kids, I was struck by the fact that none of them said that it was never okay to snoop. One explained:

It depends on the kid, and unless parents are being paranoid or overly protective, I think they know if they can trust their kid or not. If the kid is basically a good kid, let them figure out who they can be friends with, and even if they start acting like the bad kids, sometimes they need to do a couple of stupid things before they realise that they don't want to go down that road. Give them some space.

There was dissent among these teenagers about how far to let kids travel down the road into dangerous behaviours, but they all agreed that when parents attempt to control teenagers' social lives their children are much more likely to become deceptive.

"My friends with strict parents lie so much more than the kids whose parents let them have some freedom."

"Yeah, this one friend of mine, her parents think she's perfect and doing everything they tell her to do, but she's lying to them about *everything*, even stuff she doesn't have to lie about."

There were nods all around.

Adolescent psychologist Jennifer Hartstein stresses the importance of finding a way to support, but not control, teens through their adolescent relationships:

Adolescence is a time when friendships are the toughest, in many ways. Teens are learning who they are, what they want and how to balance that with friends experiencing the same things. It is so valuable to encourage adolescents to be interpersonally effective on their own, as they will soon be leaving home and need to do so in many aspects of their lives. For parents, this is a huge challenge, as seeing their teen in pain or struggling is terrifying. Be a guide and a safe place for problem solving, rather than the problem solver. Your teen will gain strength from knowing that he/she faced a problem with a peer directly and handled it, learning what works and what doesn't along the way, and thus being more prepared for all the challenges adulthood presents.

Yes, kids will make bad choices in friends, and some friendships will fail, but in retrospect these experiences enable us to recognise the traits of a healthy relationship versus a toxic one. As hard as it is to live up to Hartstein's challenge, the rewards – independent, courageous and brave young adults who understand what they want and need from the friends they will make and rely on over a lifetime – are worth the restraint and patience.

I recognise, however, that the stakes are higher once kids hit adolescence. A failed relationship or social interaction as an eight-year-old is much less traumatic than a hormone-fuelled adolescent feud and much less worrying than teenage problems involving drugs, alcohol, drink driving and eating disorders. That said, here are some tools for meeting Hartstein's challenge while protecting your child's safety and emotional health.

If your child changes in ways that make you uncomfortable as a result of his friendships, talk to him about what he likes or is drawn to in these new friends. "What do you like about Mike? What do you two do together? You seem to be spending a lot of time with Mike; what is it that you find interesting in him?" Even if Mike grates on your very last nerve, offer to host Mike more often, not less, so you will have a better understanding of your child's relationship. Make sure your son understands that your expectations for his behaviour have not changed, and that your house rules will extend to Mike, but that he is welcome in your home.

Having a problematic kid over to your house also gives you the opportunity to get to know the proverbial enemy and understand what you are dealing with. At best, you will find that your son's new friend is a really great person who wants what's best for your son and their relationship. At worst, your suspicions will be confirmed, and you will have evidence you can point to in your discussions with your child about why he is no longer allowed to have that kid over to your house anymore.

Offer to drive your son and his friend around. There's something about car trips that elicits unguarded conversation. It's as if the kids forget you are there and open up their inhibitions and conversational topics. Listen and look in the rearview mirror. Use these visits and car trips as a way to get to know the parents of these friends. You may find that these parents who hold different views to you, or you may find allies who want the same things for their child that you want for yours. In the end, remember that you do not have the power to change other people's children. You can only make your expectations clear and follow through with consequences when those expectations are breached.

- Don't lecture. Children, and particularly adolescents, will tune out the moment you start. Take it from a teacher. If your communication style tends toward lecturing, you are going to have to change it, because you cannot force your child to start listening.
- Ask an open-ended question and then listen. "Kevin seems different from your other friends. How did you guys become friends?" would be a great non-judgmental, non-threatening opener that gently cracks open the door for further conversation.
- If unsafe behaviour is the topic, try talking about

the safety issue rather than simply passing judgment on the friends. Kids get defensive and protective of their relationships the moment it seems as if their friends are being attacked. Best to stick with facts and actions as opposed to character assassination.

Adolescents have a heightened sense of loyalty, and will defend their friends' behaviour even when they feel uncomfortable about it. Stick with what you know about your own child's behaviour, and if she has acted wisely in the face of a dangerous or problematic situation, make sure to praise her for her judgment and fortitude – with a statement such as "It must have been hard for you to say no to that party last week when all your friends were there, but you knew it was liable to get out of hand. I'm really proud of you for saying no."

Once, when I shared my own worries about sending my teenager out into the world, an older mother who had been listening in on my conversation shared her personal lightbulb moment, one I've tried to keep with me every time I watch my son head out the door. She said,

One time my teenage son was going somewhere, I don't know where, and I said on the way out the door "be careful," as I always had. I then heard my husband say, "Have fun," and for the first time, I heard the differences in our parenting approaches summed up in that one exchange. My kid had always been a careful kid, and my words, whether I said them or not, were not going to serve as some magic charm over his experience. All he heard was that I did not trust him to be careful, whereas his father did. That was the last time I ever said, "Be careful," as he left the house with friends.

As we send our kids out into the world, we need to trust them more, and when they live up to our trust, catch them doing things right and praise them. This may require changing your mindset but keep an eye out for their good judgment, character and resilience, and let them know that that's what you value above all else. Make sure they know that if events spiral out of control, and they find themselves in a dangerous or threatening situation, you will help, no questions asked... until the next day. Hold your comments about how on earth they ended up smoking a cigarette at the Year 9 disco or sitting in the passenger seat of a car with a drunk driver. Once they are safe, and have had a good night's sleep, discuss the specifics of what happened and why. Using poor judgment is part of growing up. If they had the presence of mind to call you for help, focus on the fact that they respected and trusted you enough to say no to a situation they sensed was unsafe; now live up to that trust and help them figure out how not to get into that situation again.

Model positive and mutually beneficial friendships for your children. Talk about what makes a good friend and why you consider your friends good influences in your life. Ask them how they think their friends describe them. Oh, and one extra tip: eradicate toxic and harmful people from your own life before fixing your sights on the toxic and harmful elements in your children's lives, because your example is going to teach them much more about the anatomy of healthy relationships than your words ever will.

If, however, all of this careful communication and planning goes nowhere and you continue to have worries about your child's relationships, the time may come when it's appropriate to intervene. First, check your motives. Are you truly interested in the safety of your child, or are you looking for ammunition on kids you fear are bad influences in your child's life? If so, step back, take a breath, and stay out of it.

If you are still worried, try these alternatives before snooping and breaking your child's trust:

- Talk to other adults, the teacher, administrators, and coaches, and find out if the child in question is really a bad influence.
- If you can, meet the friend's parents in person and gently sound them out.
- Talk to your child about behaviour you have witnessed that makes you uncomfortable.
- If it becomes clear that this kid is a bad influence, based on actual evidence rather than fear, do your best to limit time with this friend e.g. by finding attractive alternative things to do. Keep in mind that this can backfire, and your child will react poorly to any explicit attempts to control his social life.

If you are still concerned, and have done that gut check to make sure your motives are pure and centred on the health and safety of your child, here are some examples of circumstances that warrant snooping:

- Sudden changes in behaviour, personality, weight, sleep patterns, or general health.
- Changes in your child's communication patterns. To some extent, of course, this is just part and parcel of adolescence but if your child is usually willing to

share with you, has she suddenly stopped doing so? Conversely, if your child never was a big talker, is he suddenly trying to tell you something? If so, make sure you are listening.

- Evidence of drugs or alcohol use (drug paraphernalia, suspicions that your child is drunk or high).
- Changes in academic results or studying habits.

If any of the above circumstances arise at your home, it might be time to take a look into your child's room, social networks, or simply Google your child's name and see what comes up.

If you stumble upon something that needs to be dealt with immediately, such as information that your child or your child's friends might be in danger, certainly act on that information. However, if the situation is not life-threatening, hold off for a while. Give your child time and perhaps he will confide in you. Also allow for the possibility that sometimes, even with proof, you can misconstrue what is happening in your child's life.

If your child is in trouble, or at risk of dangerous behaviours, or any number of the pitfalls that come up in a teenager's life, remember that you have the power to align yourself with your child and help him cope. Keep autonomy, love and support at the forefront of your priorities so as not to risk alienating yourself from your child and losing the opportunity to save him from peril. At the first sign of drug or alcohol abuse, eating disorders, or self-injury, seek professional help rather than attempt to handle the situation yourself.

Above all else, do not promise your child that you can "fix" his problems, social or otherwise. You may not be able to and it's important that your child understands that not everything can be magically remedied with a wave of the parental wand. Some problems are too big for that, and some require complex and imperfect solutions.

Fortunately, if parents have done their jobs right, kids will have the competence and courage to face these complex and imperfect solutions. As much as I wanted to grow up as Anne of Green Gables with a nut-brown-haired Diana Barry as my best friend, I didn't. I had complicated and often fraught friendships with the children in my neighbourhood. We were the fortunate prisoners of each other's constant company, and we had to cobble out our own treaties and lines of demarcation across the boundaries of our comfort zones. This is childhood. Those shifting, hotly contested and embattled lines, littered with successes and failures, don't just define childhood boundaries; they define the people our children will become, and we owe them the time and space they require to explore those territories.

7

SPORTS: LOSING AS AN ESSENTIAL CHILDHOOD EXPERIENCE

Wherever groups of parents congregate, discussion quickly turns to our children, and a recent breakfast with friends was no exception. The school year was just beginning, and the subject of sport came up. I had heard the horror stories before. Sports are too competitive, parents scream at children from the sidelines, and coaches dole out trophies for simply showing up. When the tone shifted from indignant to upset, and the stories took a turn I didn't expect, I finally understood who the real losers are in this era of hyper-competitive sports specialisation: kids who just want to play. Here's one mom's tale of woe, told over that breakfast:

I always loved sports, and when I was little, sports were where I established my identity, so I was thrilled when I finally convinced my daughter to get out there and give sports a shot. But instead of finding fun and exercise and identity, she's found that she's too late. Even the recreational league is so intense that the coaches won't work with her or let her play. We tried gymnastics, but those kids have been training since they were toddlers, so that didn't work out either. She wants to try some different sports and see what she likes, but everything is so *serious* now that she can't just try stuff out. She's nine. Isn't nine when you are supposed to be playing a lot of different sports and figuring out what you like to do?

This mom was almost in tears by the time she finished speaking, and the room fell silent. No one had any good suggestions for her, and everyone knew that what she was saying was true. Another mom concurred: "It's frustrating because I just want my kids to try out lots of things, learn some sports or dance basics, and have fun, but the machine of youth sports is wound so tight it is difficult to break in."

> Somewhere along the line we got distracted, and the playing field became the dinner table of the new millennium.

We don't live in a particularly intense or competitive community, yet by the time the kids hit nine or ten, many have been specialising in a sport for a couple of years. The local indoor soccer league actually starts at age three with their "Tykes" league.

How about a league called "I just wanna play"?

Talking to administrators and teachers in a number of schools all I found was further confirmation that childhood sports are no longer about play. A high school basketball coach lamented, "If only my players wanted to do it as badly as their parents do." For many kids and their parents, sports have become as much, if not more, about planning for their university applications than about fun and exercise. Competition for the top spots in high school and college sports in America is becoming so intense, it's no wonder children are stressed out and under great pressure to perform at younger and younger ages.

Dr Louis Profeta, author and emergency medicine physician in Indiana who treats these young athletes' repetitive motion stress injuries, wonders why we impose this pressure on our kids and sacrifice so much of what used to define family time:

> Somewhere along the line we got distracted, and the practice field became the dinner table of the new millennium. Instead of huddling around a platter of baked chicken, mashed potatoes and fruit salad, we spend our evenings handing off our children like 4 x 200 batons. From baseball practice to cheerleading, from swimming lessons to personal training, we have become the "hourlong" generation of five to six, six to seven, and seven to eight, selling the souls of our family for lacrosse tryouts.

The degradation of the idea of play for the sake of play, the disruption of family time, the unnecessary pressure placed on kids of all ages are all hugely problematic issues when it comes to childhood sports, but we are forgetting that one of the most significant aspects of sports is as an arena to learn about and accept failure.

Sports psychologist Terry Orlick refers to youth sports programmes as "failure factories", and if this is the case, why do we pretend that every one of the 40 million American children who play youth sports should emerge from each game a winner? If kids are inevitably going to face failure and losses in sports programmes, why not embrace it? Imagine if sports could be a safe place to fail, where athletes and teams could lose and the aftermath would be all about sportsmanship rather than conflict over that last contested call or doomsday panic about the child's future. Sports should be the place and time to experience disappointment and failure in a lower-stakes environment, a brief window of time to lay down the foundation our children will need in order to grow into adults of character.

The benefits of sports off the field

In *The Parents We Mean to Be: How Well-Intentioned Adults Undermine Children's Moral and Emotional Development*, psychologist Richard Weissbourd describes the empathy and appreciation that can be developed in children through sports:

> Competition challenges children to appreciate the skills of opposing players even when they seem like mortal enemies, to find weaker team-mates' strengths even when those players are jeopardising the team's chances of making the play-offs, to take the referee's perspective, at least after the game, even when he or she makes a bad call at a critical moment. That's the kind of demanding morality that helps to develop over time children's capacity to see beyond their own intense feelings, to tolerate others' flaws, to place others' perspectives and needs on a par with their own.

Sports also offer parents the gift of time with their children. Most sports participation requires a fair amount of car travel to practices and tournaments, and in my experience, this is where some of the most honest and unguarded conversations with my teenage son take place. So much of parenting is about being there when our kids decide they want to talk to us. I have also found that the more positive and relaxed the atmosphere in the car, the more often kids will seize the opportunity to talk about difficult subjects, topics that are not likely to come up in the usual course of a stressful, task-orientated and tightly scheduled day. Here is a place to talk about the ups and downs of what happened at the game or at practice, a place to confide in disappointments, exhaustion, passion or disinterest.

Unfortunately this is not the case for the majority of families, as Bruce Brown and Rob Miller, two former coaches who now run Proactive Coaching LLC, discovered. Over the course of twelve years, Brown and Miller conducted an informal survey of athletes about what makes supportive and effective sports parents. When Brown asked college athletes, "'What is your worst memory from playing youth and high school sports?' their overwhelming response was, 'The ride home from games with my parents.'" Teens across the country are apparently sharing tense car rides home from games with parents who use the hours of travel time to criticise players, second-guess coaches, and deride referees. That's a lot of valuable parenting opportunity wasted, hours that could be used for conversation and the enjoyment of each other's company.

In an illustrative corollary to this finding, this study revealed who kids *really* want at their games and, presumably, in the car on the way home: grandparents. Grandparents don't criticise or micromanage in the moments after the game. Grandparents don't critique the coach's strategy or a referee's call. Even in the face of embarrassing failures on the field, grandparents support their grandchildren with no ulterior motive or agenda. So if you want to become the kind of person your child wants to be around after the big game, act more like a grandparent. When your kids have kids, do you imagine your response to a missed goal will be to criticise and berate your grandchildren, or are you simply going to enjoy being around them? My mother is fond of telling me that the most wonderful thing about having grandchildren is that grandparents get to enjoy the fun parts (like watching sports practice) without the anxiety and stress over the grandchild's performance. Try, fail, succeed, she doesn't care, she just wants to be there, cheering her grandchildren on through all of it. Wouldn't it be a relief to enjoy the fun parts *now*, instead of a generation down the line, and let the coach be the one in charge of how your child and his team perform at the big game? It's not an impossible dream. Let the coach be the coach, let the referee be the referee, and when it comes time for your child to play, step back and be more like a grandparent.

Pressured parents on the sidelines

When parents intensify competition through hovering, yelling, berating, and secondguessing players, coaches, and referees, everyone loses. Kids are miserable, coaches are driven crazy, and all that stress can't be making parents very happy, either. If you are one of these unhappy parents, you should know that the monster that emerges on the sidelines lives in all of us and is part of our basic biology.

143

Psychologist Wendy Grolnick refers to this response as "Pressured Parents Phenomenon":

> The PPP is a visceral anxiety, triggered when the ever-increasing competition – academic, athletic, social or artistic – that our kids face today switches on our physiological hardwiring. It's an internal pressure so strong that we can't rest until we feel our child is safe – has gained admission to that certain magnet school or won a spot in the school orchestra [or made the university team].

The problem with feeling these completely natural feelings, Grolnick explains, is that "it alienates our children from us – a result exactly opposite of what we intended. Because, ironically, it's the absence of pressure that allows our kids to both remain close to us and to succeed." However, when we see our kids under stress, even if it's just the pressure to hit a homerun, our fight-or-flight reflex kicks in. Your brain may know your kid is not in danger, but your body goes into high alert mode and cortisol levels go sky high. Once PPP kicks in, and our stress hormones start flowing, it can be really difficult to calm down and find the lessons in failure. PPP heightens emotions and our sense of crisis, so in those moments on the sidelines when our parental anxiety and competition begin to spiral, it's especially important to recognise your surroundings for what they are: a game. Close your eyes if you have to, but relax. The reason children start playing sports in the first place is to have fun, exercise, and learn the invaluable lessons of sportsmanship and teamwork. This should still be the goal, even when the stakes get higher and aspirations of glory are on the line.

Parenting and competition can be a terrible mix, particularly when parents pit siblings against each other. In his book *Drive*, Daniel Pink recommends that work teams be a "no competition" zone. "Pitting coworkers against one another in the hope that competition will spark them to perform better rarely works – and almost always undermines intrinsic motivation." Families, like offices and classrooms, are best conducted in the absence of the stress of competition.

Competition, in turn, encourages over-parenting, even when the competition is for approval rather than trophies or scholarships. In one study, mother-child pairs were told to complete an "About Me" questionnaire. Half of the pairs were told to complete the form "for fun", while the mothers in the other half were told that their children would be meeting a group of kids who would use the form to "rate" their children. The first group of mothers, the ones who had no expectation that their child would be assessed, sat back and watched their child fill out the form on their own. However, the mothers who believed their children would be rated and scrutinised, pressured their child to fill in answers that might help the child look good and be liked by the other kids. The very idea that their child would be rated or measured against other children caused those mothers to over-parent.

After seeing her five children through active careers in amateur sports, one mother admitted to me that she had actively dissuaded her sixth child from going the same route. "I just could not take it anymore," she admitted. "I had spent years cheering and supporting, and I know that sports are a great way to stay fit and teach teamwork, but I could not take one more afternoon of competitive sniping on the sidelines. The lessons and the trophies are great, and I was happy my other kids got to experience that, but I was done with it all."

This mother would be happy to know that even the upsides she recounts, such as trophies and awards, may not be as positive as we are led to believe. Those trophies, medals, and scholarships that we dangle as reward for our children's athletic efforts don't just heighten a sense of competition and anxiety, they undermine drive. Just as rewards for positive behaviours are intrinsic motivation killers in academic and social contexts, they also dampen participation and enthusiasm in sports and other recreational activities.

In one study, researchers asked kids ages nine to eleven to play on a stabilometer, a device that measures balance and had proven to be a lot of fun for kids of that age. Half of the children received a reward for playing on the stabilometer, and the other half did not. A few days later, these kids were asked to come back and play some more, and they were given a variety of options for play, including access to the stabilometer. The kids who had been rewarded the first time around spent less time on the device than the children who had played on it for their own personal enjoyment in the first play session. This is a good example of how rewards diminish enjoyment and motivation even in fun, non-competitive recreational activities without an obvious goal or endpoint.

I'm not proposing that we should eliminate competition and rewards altogether. There needs to be a balance. And, certainly, the practice of giving all children trophies simply because they show up on the playing field is equally harmful to a child's sense of self-worth. Parents need to find their own happy medium between the empty praise of participation trophies and the competitive drive that sacrifices their child's sportsmanship, performance, and motivation. I asked Hannah Kearney, two-time Olympic medallist in freestyle skiing, to describe the ideal sports parent:

> The perfect sports parents would be ones you never hear from the sidelines. They should be there after the game, to be supportive, when the heartbreaking things happen. Kids get cut from the team, they get injured, that's just what happens in sports, but the perfect sports parent is there after that heartbreak to listen and help the kid find the positive in the heartbreak. I have to admit, my parents bribed me when I was ten with a pair of soccer shorts in order to get me to commit to my first week of practice, and I remember the adrenaline of that first goal. From that first goal on out, I was committed to sports, and they were there for me. My mom and dad sacrificed everything for my ski career and my brother's hockey. My mom drove me back and forth to Waterville Valley [a ski area in New Hampshire], held up my boom box on the mountainside so I could hear my music while I practised routines, she choreographed those routines, and copied pages from my textbooks so I could do my homework when I was traveling. They were supportive, but they never pushed me. After a kid finds a sport they love, it has to be up to the kid to go forward, or it's a disaster for everyone.

A guide to successful sideline parenting

In order to be that parent who can help a child find the positive in the heartbreak, Kearney and the other athletes, coaches and sports parents I interviewed offer the following guidelines:

Be the parent, not the coach

Unless your child's safety is at risk, don't yell from the side-lines, don't criticise coaching decisions or referee calls in the car after the game, and don't do any armchair coaching in the living room. Feel free to talk with the coach about ways to help your child improve, how your child behaves during practices or games, or ways to troubleshoot issues around injuries, but do not discuss other children on the team, team strategy, or your own child's playing time.

Never, ever, criticise the coach in front of your child

This destroys your child's trust, respect and faith in his coach and creates a real emotional dilemma for him. If he agrees with you, he's betraying his coach and if he agrees with his coach, he's betraying you. Don't put him in that position. Talk to, and about, the coach only when your child is not around to hear it.

Don't ask your child to fulfil your own athletic dreams

It does not matter how talented you were in softball, soccer, or chess when you were a kid; your child is not you. Don't be the parent who attempts to relive past glory or play out unfulfilled dreams through a child. You may love football with all your heart and soul, and put a Chelsea FC onesie on your child the moment he exits the womb, but as we are not (yet) engaging in human cloning, your child will have his own, desires, hopes and dreams. Give him a chance to figure out what those dreams are instead of imposing yours on him.

Cultivate a growth mindset with plenty of room for failure

Sports are hard, and only get harder as kids progress through the ranks. Caroline Gleich, professional skier and extreme athlete, explained that the transition from recreational athlete to professional athlete was hard for her at first because she was operating from a fixed mindset.

> I really had to change my mindset, because my parents had always told me I was great, and I'd never had to work at my sport. So with skiing, I thought there were things like ski jumps that I just could not do. I would see other people do these amazing tricks, but I figured, I'd never taken gymnastics, so I simply could never do those tricks. I had to shift from what I can't do to what I can do and I had to really work at it. That became part of the fun, to stay focused on the goal even when things get hard.

Gleich has excelled in her sport because she's come to understand that her initial failures are necessary steps toward eventual accomplishment, steps that make the final push to a mountain summit or the top of a glacier all the more rewarding.

Know the difference between quitting and failure

It's easy for successful, professional athletes to look back on their failures and moments of challenge with fondness, but what if challenges prove insurmountable and it's time to accept the fact that a career or even participation in a given sport is not to be? Michael Thompson, psychologist and author, points out that there comes a time when all of us must decide whether or not the struggle – of sports, or a relationship, or any other path we choose to take – is worth the pain. "In a broad sense, all learning and growth require struggle, but there is a difference between the experience of struggle that leads to success and the experience of struggle that leads to only more struggle." Not every child is destined to become a professional athlete, and as kids move up through the "failure factories" toward the more rarefied air of high school and regional teams, nearly all of them will have to decide when to throw in the towel. When this happens, we parents have to help our children find the value in the experience of sports, whether that's fun, fitness, or the lessons they've learned in courage, failure, resilience, sportsmanship and teamwork. These lessons are not lost just because they stop playing the game. I've heard many parents say "I can't let my kid be a quitter," or "I have to teach my son that you follow through on your obligations to the team" as reasons to force children to play when they no longer love a sport. However, as K. C. Potts, basketball coach and English teacher told me, this approach can be a mistake:

> The tragedy of youth sports is that kids are often signed up with little or no sense of what playing the sport entails, and when the child has the epiphany – "I don't like this sport" – the parent opts to invoke the "you can't quit during the season" clause and force the child to stick with it. There is the nobility

of following through with a "commitment", yes, but often younger children have not really made a commitment, and the parents' insistence brings misery to everyone: to the coach who must find time for a player who does not want to play, to the parents who believe that they are somehow building the character of a child who in their eyes does not have enough, and most of all to a child who plays not for enjoyment but out of some obligation. Nobody smiles, nobody wins.

Sports are, after all, supposed to be fun. This was the number one sentiment I heard in all the stories shared by successful athletes. The bottom line is that they love their sport and have fun with it, even in practice. As they progress from team to team, and league to league, or give up sports completely, children rely on parents to anchor their family team and provide the kind of unwavering support that can help them through their most humiliating and humbling failures. In those moments, they need us to remind them that as long as they show up on the field and do their very best, in sports or anywhere else, we will keep up our end of the bargain and show up on the sidelines to cheer them on.

8

EARLY TEENS: PRIME TIME FOR FAILURE

Y ou teach 11-14 year-olds? Really?"
The question is usually punctuated by a wince, and a look of pity.

Yes, it's true. I happily spend eight hours a day in the company of "tweens," a much misunderstood and maligned population well versed in the everyday business of academic and social failures. Even among my peers – educators who understand the joys and rewards inherent in teaching – the early secondary school classroom is often viewed as educational and professional purgatory. When I asked parents for their positive sentiments about the early teens, one mother's submission spoke for the group: "I think I need some distance from this era before I find my anecdotes entertaining."

I wholeheartedly disagree.

Of course young adolescents are challenging. They are going through a time of enormous change. There are days when I can't imagine these mere children will ever be prepared to enter the world on the world's terms; they are demanding, curious, impulsive and mercurial, and they can be maddening. But these same maddening traits are the very tools that will allow them to navigate the tricky waters of the teenage years and emerge as more fully formed people.

Here's the ugly and wonderful truth about American middle school: it's a set-up. Middle school teachers ask 11-14 year-olds students to succeed at tasks that their half-cooked, adolescent brains are not yet able to master, and therefore, failure is not an *if* proposition, it's a matter of when. This is one of the first truths I tell my students, because the sooner they accept this reality, the easier everyone's life. It's true of Years 7-9 in British secondary schools too. The students are given a level of responsibility and autonomy that is initially very challenging. Some kids really love this challenge, and rise to it as if it's been what they have been waiting for all their lives.

> The best part of my transition from the equivalent of primary to secondary school was the idea that you were responsible for your own actions. In primary school, teachers were always reminding you to hand your homework in, hang your coat up, pay attention, and stay organised. In a sense, Year 6 had been spent preparing ourselves for the daunting prospect of secondary school and so to finally get there was rewarding in itself.

For young people like this, who are ready, the opportunity to have control over their lives is exciting. For others, the transition is not quite so easy. British secondary school demands feats of organisation, planning, time management and shifts of focus that young adolescents are not capable of mastering, at least not all at once. Some kids can handle one or two of these skills some of the time, but for most students, genuine mastery of all of them doesn't come for a couple of years. Think about it this way: infants can't yet speak because their brains are not sufficiently developed to master the complex physical tasks of forming language. Toddlers can't plan and execute long term projects because their brains have not yet made the neurological connections that allow for long term planning and sequenced execution of complex tasks. We don't expect little kids to be able to do these things, but we do expect young teenagers to be able to handle the complexity of secondary school, even though they, too, are still lacking the neurological connections that will allow them to manage the demands we place on them.

It can be really hard to remember this, particularly when, thanks to the vagaries of puberty, some students are rapidly starting to look like hulking adults. I've taught classes where pre-pubescent babyfaced children study alongside man-sized boys who need to shave every day. Despite all appearances, those physically advanced kids are still children as far as their brains are concerned, and it's important to remember this while we patiently wait for their neurons to catch up with their five o'clock shadow.

When students stumble in on the first day of school, the faculty is ready for them. We spend the first couple of months watching them shove crumpled papers into lockers, helping them pick up the scattered remains of binder explosions, and suggesting ways to remember what class comes after English and what materials to take to science. One mother explains the chaos of this stage like this: "I fear for my hands every time I reach into his backpack. I don't know what is in there. Neither does he."

Learning to organise, plan and conquer "what's in there" takes a concerted effort from students, parents and teachers and even I have my moments of doubt. I worry for their future. I worry that I have precious little time to prepare them for the more complicated and challenging world after they leave. I can never see how there will be enough time to get them ready, but there almost always is. Somehow, that chronically late, perennially disorganised Year 7 boy who can't use a diary for two days in a row is able to manage his academic life by the time I wave goodbye to him.

So fear not. Failure is a fact of life in those early years of secondary school, so embrace it. Everyone is doing it, even the cool kids. Even the children who look as though they have it all figured out. The stakes are still low, and teachers understand that small disasters happen every hour of every day, so jump in and take advantage of all those learning experiences in the guise of everyday failures.

The name of the game is executive function

The elusive skills that students will need to survive in high school and life are part and parcel of what psychologists call *executive function*, or the collection of skills and mental processes that allow us to manage our time, resources and attention in order to achieve a goal. There are many skills that make up executive function, and I would argue that the diagnosis "executive function deficit" is merely a synonym for "early adolescence". Failure to engage or access executive function skills is what causes most secondary school disasters such as forgotten homework, missing P.E. kits and lost textbooks. An understanding of this root cause is the first step toward maintaining some perspective on this otherwise frustrating and maddening period in your child's academic life. This understanding also gives you a step up on all those other frustrated parents, as they worry and search the heavens for answers as to where they went wrong. Best of all, you will be able to respond to the inevitable failures your child will encounter as a result of executive function deficits and teach her how to avoid repeating her mistakes.

While it's tempting to blame executive function deficits on a lack of intelligence, don't go there; they are not related. Executive function skills develop as the adolescent brain develops, and all we can do as teachers and parents is support kids as they learn from their mistakes. Executive function skills develop at different rates, and while some kids acquire them quickly, others continue to have issues throughout life. It's not coincidental that the students whose parents bail them out, and don't allow them to deal with the consequences of these failures, develop these skills more slowly.

The key to helping kids create the systems they need to gain executive function is to let them fail, let them feel the pain and inconvenience of their mistakes, and then support them in their efforts to rework the bugs. Try, fail, suffer a little, remedy, try again. Over and over again until they learn. A few missed lunches or a zero on the homework left on the kitchen table will reinforce these skills better than your lectures or nagging ever will. Every intervention or rescue is a lesson lost. They need every minute, every learning opportunity that we can grant them before they face the much greater challenges and consequences that await them in life after school.

While you are waiting for your child's brain to develop,

here's a rundown on the collection of skills and habits that constitute the umbrella definition of executive function, plus tips on strengthening those skills and supporting your child while he struggles with solutions and fails in their execution.

The struggle for self-control

One lovely spring day, while I was preparing my English class notes and the class was settling in to their desks, I felt something whizz past my head and hit the whiteboard behind me. I whirled around, trying to figure out why I was under attack, and realised that someone had thrown a mechanical pencil at me. One glance up at the class, and it was obvious who was the culprit. His eyes were wide, his mouth was hanging open, and he was doing his very best to avoid my stare. After class, I took him aside and asked him what he had been thinking.

"Well, I wasn't *aiming* at your head," he said. "I was aiming at the recycling bin."

"But a mechanical pencil isn't even recyclable... No. Wait. Hold on. Let's back up. What were you *thinking* just before you threw the pencil at me?"

He looked at his feet and shuffled them around a bit. "Nothing." He looked up at me and shrugged again. "I didn't know I was going to throw the pencil until I'd thrown it, and by then, it was too late."

It was an honest answer. The key to helping kids curb their impulsive behaviour is to teach them how to understand their patterns of conduct and the body language that tends to precede these behaviours. We have to catch adolescents *before* they throw the pencil or paper airplane, point out their jiggling leg or twitching fingers, in order to teach them to recognise these signs as precursors of problematic behaviours. Adolescents are notoriously lacking in self-awareness, but if we point out the precursor behaviour often enough, they will learn to recognise the signs themselves and redirect their focus. It's not easy; it's one of the greatest challenges teachers face when juggling the needs of twenty or more children at a time, but teaching self-awareness is an important part of helping kids gain control of their own behaviour.

Even for that kid who threw that pencil at my head. It took a while, but even he managed to leave school with a pretty good sense of self-control and the ability to recognise when he was beginning to lose it. There were plenty of failures along the way, but I like to think his teachers and parents helped him find a lesson in many of them.

Here are some techniques that can help kids gain some self-control and awareness of their own patterns of disruptive or distracting behaviours.

Agree on a signal

For some of my students, a light tap on the shoulder is all they need in order to regain focus and composure. Before class, when the mood is light and the student is feeling positive, I take her aside and propose that we come up with a mutually agreed upon signal. It can be a word, a tap on the shoulder, or a look, whatever the student wants. When I notice the student losing focus or beginning to show signs of an impending impulsive behaviour, I take a casual stroll around the room and invoke our signal. It's an amazingly effective strategy, one that can work at home as well. It saves the child from embarrassment, and can be a way to communicate without nagging or shouting.

The Pencil Game

Child psychologist William Hudenko taught me a technique that can help kids learn how to recognise signs of impending impulsive behaviours, and then signal to their brain that they need to refocus. Give the child a set of two or three pencils and teach him to switch pencils when he feels his brain getting distracted. It's not really about which pencil he uses, but switching pencils gives his brain the prompt, "Oh, I'm distracted, I need to get focused again." Switching pencils becomes the signal for his brain to refocus. Eventually, he won't need the pencils, because his brain will learn to recognise distraction and he will begin to automatically redirect his focus, but in the beginning, the pencils offer a way to become conscious of subtle signals of distraction.

FER

Hudenko also suggests another technique he calls "FER," which stands for Flag, Eye contact and Rehearse. "Flag," according to Hudenko, means to "figure out what's important to pay attention to"; for instance, if a teacher is talking in class, the student should listen for the highlights he thinks are important. "Eye contact" means, literally, that he should be making eye contact with whoever is speaking. Finally, "rehearse" means to repeat, or rehearse the important points in his mind, so they will get moved from short-term to long-term memory. This process is really for attention issues, but it also gives the student something to focus on, which helps head off impulsive behaviours.

All of these techniques will take time, practice and patience, and there will be lots of failures along the way. The important thing to remember is that talking about the process of being in control and coming up with a plan such as the pencil game or FER will at least set the stage for an awareness of this issue.

Limbering up for mental flexibility

If I were to walk into my son's room while he is deep into the construction of an imaginary kingdom and announce that we will be departing in five minutes for an amusement park, he'd complain about having to stop playing with his blocks. It's not that he doesn't want to go to the amusement park; he would not hear what I was saying. All he would hear was that there would be a change, and he wouldn't like it. It would take him a minute or two to make the switch from blocks to roller-coaster.

At five, this cognitive inflexibility is par for the course, but once your child gets to eleven, he is going to have to learn how to switch mental gears many times a day.

One of the most difficult transitions for tweens is the shift from home to school. Adolescents, and particularly young adolescents, need quite a bit of time in the morning to wake up and prepare for the day. When your child barely makes it to school on time, he is being put at a major disadvantage. Kids really need a good ten or fifteen minutes to empty their backpacks, reorganise their materials, talk to their friends, adjust their outfits, and get their heads on straight before first period. Without this time of transition, that first class is a nightmare for them. Their brains, bodies, and belongings will be disorganised, and many of these kids don't really pull themselves together until lunchtime, when they get a moment to breathe, unpack and arrange their priorities for the day.

Once he is at school, he will have to move between classes and subjects, reorient his brain from maths to French, go to his locker for the correct textbook, and adjust to various teachers, all with their own rules, expectations and personalities. A simple illustration of this sort of mental inflexibility arose a few years ago when my 12-year-old Latin students came to my class straight from French class. The word for "and" is spelled the same way in both languages, *et*, but it is pronounced "eh" in French and "et" in Latin. Students who never normally mispronounced were suddenly dropping their t's all over the place when they arrived straight from French. It became a running joke that year, but the following year when Latin was no longer timetabled after French, the mistake disappeared as if it had never existed.

Even after they survive the many transitions in their school day, kids are then faced with shifting gears between one extracurricular and another. They must navigate the mental leaps from football training to homework, from dinner to reading in bed. If they were not already exhausted from the school day leaps, they certainly will be by the time their heads hit the pillow. The sheer mental exhaustion of these leaps of focus, paired with the massive amounts of academic, physical and social data adolescents are expected to assimilate and process every day, require that they get plenty of sleep.

Here are practical guidelines for helping your child manage transitions:

- Create some predictability in your household. Continuity and predictability aren't just reassuring for toddlers; stability calms adolescents as well.
- Keep a family calendar and try to remind kids of appointments and schedules.
- Kids should keep their own schedule as soon as they are able. When kids are aware of and organise their own timetables, they will gain a sense of autonomy, pushing them toward greater independence.
- Keep your child on a regular sleep schedule, even on weekends and holidays. Studies show that it takes a long time to recover from even a small shift in sleep routines, and sufficient sleep is key to almost every aspect of developing executive function.
- When unexpected changes come up in the family's schedule, model calmness. Children feed off adult cues and learn how to manage stressful situations through their parents' examples. If you handle transitions with grace, they will be much more likely to emulate that grace.

That poor, poor working memory

If you know anything about computers, then think of working memory as RAM. Or think about the mind of a dog. My Labrador retriever can hold one task in her mind ("retrieve the paper!") for about two seconds, or until some other task enters her brain ("chase the squirrel!"). This deficit is not her fault, and it's not because she's stupid (although she is). She has poor working memory. Similarly, when I ask my son to feed the dog while his brain is occupied with guitar practice, he will walk into the kitchen and stare blankly at me, and I can tell that in the time it took for him to walk from his room to the kitchen, he's forgotten what I asked him to do. While this behaviour is irritating, it is also completely normal. A gentle reminder – best if it's handed over without irritation or judgment – will get him back on track.

A lack of working memory isn't just annoying at home; it's a real problem for kids in school. Teachers tend to give students oral information, and if the student can't keep that information in mind long enough to write it down in her notebook or planner, that information is lost forever... or until the student asks the teacher to repeat it and gets a dirty look for "not listening the first time round". When I give my students an assignment, I try to look them in the eyes and wait until they are paying full attention. Even then, I will inevitably have to repeat the assignment a couple of times, particularly if it contains specific details such as page numbers. In order to retain my sanity, I write it down for them on a chalkboard. Between the oral and visual command, the assignment will usually make it into their diaries.

Here are some practical strategies for 11-14-year-old school kids with poor working memory:

- Have your child's hearing tested. Hearing and working memory are unrelated, but children with hearing deficits often look a lot like children with memory impairment, so check that off the list first thing.

- Be patient. Repetition is key, and even though that can get old really fast, try to remember that you are dealing with a developing brain.
- Write tasks down so your child can refer back to your instructions.
- If your child's school allows it, look into audio-recording classes on a dictaphone, particularly on test review days or in classes that rely on lectures to convey information.
- Teach your child critical listening skills. Part of improving working memory is filtering out all of the stuff kids don't need to remember. If you listen to the news on the radio on the way to school, ask your child, "What do you think were the two most important ideas in that story?" This skill will really pay off down the road as kids get older and the amount of information they are expected to assimilate increases.

Awake, but not necessarily aware

Adolescents have a lot of trouble looking at their own efforts and gauging their results against what is being required of them. Teachers know that in order to receive the results we want from our students, we need to be clear about what we expect. Repeatedly. I try to be precise and painfully detailed about every aspect of my expectations, because if I am not, I risk frustration and eventual mental collapse in the face of the chaos that will ensue on due dates. When I do receive assignments that fall short of my explicit instructions, I sit down with the student and give her examples of where and how she fell short.

At home, deficits in self-awareness and monitoring may show up as shoddily executed bathroom cleaning or lunches consisting solely of Hobnobs. In my house, the problematic task is log stacking, an adventure in frustration that led to a house rule that if the wood pile falls over, the person who stacked it has to do the job all over again. Wood stacking is an exhausting and splinter prone job, so it only took one or two stack collapses for my older son to perfect his wood-stacking technique. But let me repeat: adolescents require detailed and explicit guidance on their execution of a given task. I did not just send my kid outside with an IKEA-esque instructional packet or some loose oral directions; I stacked with him. I taught him how to properly form support towers at the end of the stack, account for the angle of the ground underneath the pile, and compensate for unevenly split wood. He gained an education in wood stacking, and I scored a day with my son, watching as he earned a sense of competence in the completion of a complex and challenging task.

Here are some tips for shoring up adolescents' self-awareness and their ability to gauge their progress on tasks:

- Make expectations crystal clear, from the start. Ideally, do the task with them the first time they attempt it, and offer tricks and tips for getting the task right.
- When kids claim they are finished with a task, help them compare your (or teachers') expected results with their actual results.
- If they make mistakes or fail at the task, teach them step-by-step how to remedy the situation. The way to capitalise on failures is to turn them into an education in resourcefulness and remedy. Sometimes, the

failure becomes a lesson in and of itself in another skill. Go with the flow, and teach the lessons as they emerge with patience and a sense of humour.

- Praise effort while supporting future improvement. The more kids learn how to look at their own work and measure it against external expectations, the better they will get at measuring their own progress and working up to those expectations.

Failure to launch

Kids of all ages struggle with the ability to start and get down to work on new tasks, and while this fiddling and fooling around in the face of something new looks like procrastination, psychologists call it "initiation", and it's an essential executive function skill. To initiate means to begin, to overcome entropy, launch a plan, and get down to a task. This won't come as news to any parent of an adolescent, but young teens can have trouble originating an idea, coming up with a plan for a task, and getting down to that plan, all part of executive function. Nagging seems to have the opposite of the intended effect. Sometimes it's about not being able to recognise how much time a task will take in relationship to the amount of time that's left to complete it. Sometimes it's simply a matter of inertia.

Most little kids don't initiate tasks until an adult tells them to, but as those kids get older, it will be important to transition them toward a place of independence where they initiate and complete tasks under their own power.

Here are practical tips for helping kids initiate (and follow through) on tasks:

- Encourage them to produce and maintain a clear daily, weekly, and monthly calendar. Understanding time management flows from a clear picture of how much time there is in a day and how a specific task fits into a schedule, with real deadlines and time pressure.
- Talk about time management. If a child needs to complete three tasks before bedtime, talk about how long each task might take and how much time remains in the day.
- Timers and alarm clocks can work miracles. If it works for a child to be able to watch the time run down, then do use this method – it's helpful in that it makes time a real, rather than an abstract, concept.
- .Show your kids how you budget your time. Let them see the wizard behind the curtain and understand how running a household and work life really happens. Help them understand that fully cooked meals don't just materialise in the half hour before dinner. Explain the process, figure out how long it will take to plan, shop, defrost, prepare and cook that meal, and then invite them into the process.

Organising for learning and life

Okay, this is a biggie. This is how one mother described her eleven-year-old: "My son's idea of organising his school papers is to stuff them into his locker or backpack. Every now and then he loses something important and has to complete an archeological dig through crumpled, torn, shredded papers and tests that would better be served in papier-mâché projects."

There are some practical strategies you can try in order to help your adolescent become more organised, but even if you work as a professional organiser, mastering this executive function skill is a process, not an item on a checklist to be dealt with over the short term. Many of these skills are learned over a lifetime, so adolescents are probably only going to master the rudimentary skills at first. The goal here is not perfection, but the acquisition of basic skills and strategies that will allow them to keep their papers in order, know where their test review sheet went, and understand how much time they have to study for next Friday's Latin test on the imperfect tense. This happens through trial and error, with an emphasis on the latter.

If your child's school does not teach study skills, he is going to have to learn this essential curriculum at home. Work together to come up with a method for organisation and planning. For example, every Wednesday, my students are required to empty out their lockers, organise their papers, and get their locker checked. Some of the more disorganised students are asked to take their binders into homeroom and spend ten or fifteen minutes filing away loose papers and recycling the redundant paper that seems to accumulate in the front pocket of the binder. Often, students will find that they have three copies of one assignment – the original, and the two they were given as replacements when they were *positive* that it was lost forever because they looked for it *everywhere*. If your child's school does not encourage this practice, ask him to set aside fifteen minutes a week at home to clean out and file loose papers. As your child learns to organise his materials, he won't need this extra time anymore, but fifteen minutes in the beginning is about right.

In addition to the weekly cleanout, we also schedule

some planning time once a week. Every Monday morning, we spend some time filling out work planners and transferring assignments from teachers' weekly sheets to their own calendar. My school hands out a planner specific to our calendar at the start of every year, and students are required to keep it up to date, noting all assignments and special events. Any calendar will work, though, and you should be checking over their shoulder at first in order to make sure assignments are being recorded. I make sure my students list in the appropriate boxes the names of their classes, or even better, an abbreviation that leaves lots of room for other notes, so when they need to flip to next Tuesday's French class to fill in an assignment, they can find it. The most important point here is that students should be in charge of their own schedules by the time they hit secondary school. They will need a couple of years to get used to this process, and some time to try out a few different systems to see what works for them, so give them that time. Pushing this time management responsibility off until sixth form or university is doing your kid no favours. This isn't an ability that magically appears when he needs to take on the management of his own life. It's a skill that takes practice, trial and error, and patience.

Whether your child's school has a strategy or you are flying solo at home, choose a time to organise once a week. For really bad cases, I have been known to check in on binders a couple of times a week, but a home check once a week should work. While this presents another opportunity for conflict, try to frame it as a way to see what your kid has been up to over the week. If all else fails, make it clear that you only have to do this irksome task together until your kid has a handle on his own organisational abilities. If getting Mum's nose out of a teenager's business isn't an effective reward for positive habits, I don't know what is.

A sense of humour is essential in dealing with this task. I have one student who asks me for a locker check every week, confident that he will be given the go ahead on the first try, free to head on out and play on the basketball court. I don't know where he gets this false sense of confidence, because every Wednesday for the past two years, his locker has been an unmitigated disaster. But believe it or not, this weekly date with his binders has become one of my favourite parts of the week. We find mangled papers, realise they were due yesterday, and together, we devise plans to ensure he won't make the same mistake next week. As he slowly learns, fails, then relearns expectations, we have laughed and rolled our eyes. While I will be thrilled when he finally masters his binders, I will miss that weekly bonding opportunity.

The key to learning how to organise one's materials and one's life is to try one strategy and see if it works. If it does, great; stick with what works. But if it fails, if papers are lost, deadlines are missed, and opportunities are lost as a result of flawed strategies, it's vital that the pain of that failure is felt. That pain, whether it's experienced as frustration, disappointment, sadness or anger, is what prompts change and growth. It's what prompts the formation of a new strategy, and it's what prompts learning. I hate seeing my students or my children upset, but on the other side of that upset is the promise of improvement, one more step toward the day they will be able to successfully manage their lives. Viewed in that light, failure is progress.

Parents and teachers can help adolescents develop skills to cope with deficits in these areas, but what's needed during the early years of secondary school is patience and a willingness to allow kids to deal with their failures and the consequences of their mistakes, getting detention for forgotten homework, for example. Let them fail. Let them get upset when they make mistakes, and when they do, don't save them. Every consequence experienced will hasten your child's acquisition of these skills. Conversely, every time you rescue, you extend your child's helplessness by another day.

Every time you feel tempted to drive that homework to school or make that lunch, just envision this beautiful scenario: your child packs his own bag – both for soccer and school – remembers to make *and* bring his lunch to school, makes a mental note to hand in that form you signed last night, jots some detail of a long-term project down on the calendar, and loads himself and his gear into the car without being reminded or asked. Won't that be lovely? Your kids will get there, and oh, what a beautiful world it is when they do.

9

SECONDARY SCHOOL AND BEYOND:
TOWARD REAL INDEPENDENCE

As I answered parents' questions after a school presentation on intrinsic motivation and autonomy, one
parent lurked at the back of the group, waiting patiently for
the others to ask their questions. When the last parent had
left the room, she leaned in close and whispered, "My son
is seventeen and I do *everything* for him."

She paused and held my eyes, touched my arm, and said,
once more for emphasis, "*Everything.*"

I nodded, and waited.

"I never let him fail, never, and I want to... I mean, he's
seventeen. Even if I stop now... am I too late?"

By the time she finished her question, she was squeezing
my forearm tightly, and I was pretty sure she was about to
start crying. But I could see that she was determined, so we
sat down and formulated a plan that would make the most
of the last year of her son's childhood...

We used to celebrate the end of childhood at eighteen, the traditional age of majority, when children loosened their grip on our apron strings and struck out into the world in search of independence and purpose. Over the past couple of generations, however, childhood has been lengthened by a protracted adolescence to the point where many young people enter adulthood with no idea how to function in a world that expects them to speak and act on their own behalf. Adolescent psychologist Jennifer Hartstein reports that she's increasingly seeing young people who are struggling to find their way as emerging adults:

> When these kids are not allowed to fall and pick themselves up, they never learn how to tolerate disappointment, manage their relationships, take responsibility for themselves, or cope with the anxiety of not getting what they want. I frequently pose this question to parents who are afraid to let go: "How do you expect your child to be an adult if you never let them learn how?"

Mothers and fathers are accompanying children to university open days, and even take their twenty-somethings to job interviews. As the *Journal of Adolescence* noted recently, "attempts at [parental] control are linked to negative child outcomes in emerging adulthood." The authors conclude:

> It would seem that emerging adults should be personally invested in their own growth and development by solving their own problems with roommates, making their own decisions about employment, and seeking their own help

from professors. By not doing so, emerging adults may be robbing themselves of the experiences and practice necessary to develop skills that are essential to success in marriage, careers and social interactions.

In other words, until we step back and allow teenagers to live their own lives, surviving their own failures and earning their own triumphs, they won't get a chance to experience their own sense of competence, competence they will need in order to be successful in their jobs, families and yes, even their marriages. When I asked parents with grown children about their experiences, many acknowledged just how hard it can be to let go.

> I had a terrible time letting my children fail. So much so that my son (who is now 35) wisely told me in his early teens that I had to let him fail. And to him that meant that I had to stop cringing when he did, because then he felt like his failing (rather than being a sign that he was stretching his boundaries) was a sign that he had not lived up to my expectations. He grew up believing that he should be "perfect", and "perfect" meant that he never skinned a knee and never broke a sweat.

The process of separating from us began for our children the moment we set them down on the kitchen floor and they took their first steps away from us. Every milestone – first step, first word, first day of school, first date – marks the stages of the journey toward an independent life. Our job is not to protect them from their failures along the way, but to help them cope with setbacks as they occur, because when they move out of their childhood home and begin to forge their own path, they are going to need all the resources and tools we can give them. The road ahead is theirs, not ours, and as tempted as we may be to pave the way for them so that we can live vicariously through their successes, it's time to let them live their own lives, to unravel our own priorities and needs from theirs. One very honest mother admitted how hard this can be to do: "I am a high achiever. I come from a generation of high achievers. We are the baby boomers. When my children achieve, I have reflected glory. I am confused about where they end and I begin."

The later teenage years offer parents a last chance to unravel those ties that bind our kids to helplessness, but I'm not going to sugarcoat the challenges inherent in changing course so late in in the game. If you have been a directive or controlling parent for this long, both you and your kid are used to that dynamic and it's going to take some work to undo the years of dependent routines and expectations. Teenagers, like toddlers, need a clear understanding of expectations and limits and it can be hard to move the line in the sand. When parents begin to ask more

Over the past few generations, childhood has been lengthened by a protracted adolescence to the point where many young people enter adulthood with no idea how to function on their own.

of their older kids, and stop rescuing them from the consequences of their mistakes, there will be tantrums and raging and indignation. The good news is that once the initial negativity and shock subside, it's easy to hand responsibility and consequences back to older kids because they are capable of so much. It's hard to know what tasks five or ten-year-olds can handle, but teenagers can do just about everything you can do, and sometimes better, if you give them the chance.

The hormones and emotions of adolescence make it a challenging phase of life for parents, but in terms of learning and cognitive development, it's a time of huge mental and physical gain, the perfect time to launch a full-on push toward adult competence. Teens are deep into what's known as the "formal operational stage", when they develop their ability to think more logically, deduce outcomes based on past experience and connect abstract concepts to their reality in a way they have not been able to do until now. Even more importantly, their executive function skills are more developed, so they have a new-found ability to plan for the future and come up with systems and methods for achieving the outcomes they desire. What's really fun to watch during this stage of life is the transition from the trial and error methods which younger kids use to a more strategic way of thinking about how to achieve goals. Adolescents can hold multiple possibilities and ideas in their brain at once and consider how those ideas might play out before launching willynilly into a plan. As David Bainbridge explains in his book *Teenagers: A Natural History*, "Children may be charming little people who can talk and think a little, but we do not become fully mentally human until we are teenagers."

When I talk to parents about giving kids the room to fail at this age, they claim they want to, but can't. It's just impossible these days, they argue. The stakes are too high: "It's so intense, and every grade matters!" and "I can't let [my son] fail because he only gets one shot at these public exams, and there's too much to lose." These parents argue that re-takes aren't respected, even one failure could ruin their child's chances of a place at a prestigious university. Yes, I nod, that's true, but the greater risk lies in sheltering and protecting kids from failures while they still are living at home, because failures that happen out there, in the real world, carry far higher stakes. One mother, whose children are now grown and settled in to their adult lives, pointed out that sometimes parents need to step back and consider what kind of "success" we really want for our children.

> The irony is that there are all kinds of ways to be success-ful, and they mostly boil down to being happy. If we rob our children of their opportunity to fail, we rob them of their opportunity to, ultimately, be happy despite the realities of the economic and political world they will live in because they won't develop the self-confidence and resilience necessary to find creative solutions to challenges in their own lives with their own realities.

At a recent conference of independent school guidance counsellors, one of the counsellors asked for help getting one of her young clients to understand the reasoning behind the poor grade he'd received for a plagiarised science project. The student was angry with the teacher and with his counsellor, and viewed the failing grade as an unfair punishment that put his future education at risk. His parents were furious, and had threatened to sue the school over the situation.

"I just don't understand this mentality," she told the room. "Everyone is blaming me, his teacher and the school, and no one seems to be talking about the fact that he chose to cheat. No one seems to care that this is a lesson the student needs to learn. This kid wants to be a scientist. Just imagine if he plagiarised a scientific paper in ten years' time; it would mean the end of his career. Isn't it better that he learn about the consequences of plagiarism in school rather than later?"

She was absolutely right; if we fail to teach our kids these lessons now, they will be more likely to make the same mistakes again. In adulthood, the consequences are much more serious than a poor grade or an afterschool detention. This is the last opportunity we have before our kids face the real world, with its real consequences.

Once kids are capable of adult cognition and reasoning, it's time to give them the trust, faith and responsibility they deserve.

So step back, loosen the ties, and let your older teenagers surmount the obstacles they encounter during these final four years of childhood so that they are ready to embrace adult life

The big wide world

Leaving school and the life that comes after, whether that includes further education or a job, marks a clear line in the sand. However, as childhood increasingly bleeds over into adulthood, many parents are unsure how involved they should be at this stage. The easy answer is that there are very few spheres of college life that belong to you. Your child is a legal adult, and even if you are providing financial support, it's time to stop intervening and let her suffer the consequences of her decisions and failures. Course selection, talking to professors about grades, finding accommodation, negotiating flatmate disagreements, this is all stuff your kid should handle. If she has not dealt with any of this before, now is the time to let her start.

When I asked professor Michael Chemers of University of California, Santa Cruz to elaborate on his experience with students who have been overprotected against failure and are consequently unprepared for the demands of life on their own, he replied:

> I know we've all heard horror stories about kids who show up to college without any clue how to do their laundry. I had a student in my office in tears because of this. But that's not really the problem – it doesn't take long to learn how to do your laundry. The real problem comes from the mindset of a student who emails a professor with a demand at midnight and is furious when it hasn't been addressed by 8:30am when class starts. It's when a student insists that having a real desire to do the work should earn the same grade as doing the work. It's when a college professor gets a phone call from an angry parent demanding to know why a student is failing. There's a terrible wake-up call coming, and it's not for the professor, because if your child can't write a ten-page research-based argumentative paper by his or her first year in college, it's too late. Elementary and secondary school teachers are professional *teachers*. Professors are professional *scholars* who share what they know with students as part of their agreement with the university – the rest of their commitment is to their own research and service to the university and their profession. It is not possible for a professor who is teaching a class of 300 to stay for an hour every week with each student who needs remedial help, nor is it reasonable to expect a professor to engage with a parent over every

student's particular needs or problems. In fact, the law expressly forbids us to do so without express consent from the child. On the many occasions when I have been called by an angry parent, I simply say "your child is my client; you are not. You need to speak to your child."

In order to address the voluminous requests of parents who are concerned for their children, many colleges and universities have added parent resource pages to their websites, and many others offer campus tours for parents. But just because these sorts of programmes are offered, it does not mean you have to take advantage of them. Consider which message you want to send to your child as she heads off into the world: "I did not do the job I was supposed to do when you were in my home, so now I will follow you into your adulthood to make sure you don't mess up," or "You are now an adult, and I trust you to be able to hack it in college."

Colleges and universities are actively seeking parents out and asking them to convey this message explicitly and clearly to students before they arrive on campus. The web page for parents at Northwestern University in the state of Illinois offers this reminder about what children really need from their parents during the college years:

- They need you to let go.
- They need to be able to make mistakes.
- They need to know that you believe in them.
- They need to know that you are interested, not intrusive.

I hope you started fostering your child's competence well before he left for college, but in case you are off to a late start, here are some autonomy-supportive conversations you can have in the months leading up to the start of their time at university, discussions that can help students feel in control of their university experience:

Set goals for the first year

Ask your child what he imagines the first year of college might look like, and then ask him what he could do to turn that perfect fantasy year into reality. Keep in mind that these discussions should be supportive and in the spirit of guidance rather than dictatorial and controlling.

Identify allies on campus

If she is not sure about how to reach her goals, recommend that she talk to someone who can offer guidance. Help her identify advisors, professors in areas of interest, and deans who are equipped to help. Make sure she understands the benefits of getting to know her tutors and knows how to look up the email of her professors, her advisor, or her department head, and find their offices on the campus map. All universities will offer student health and mental health services, make sure she's aware of this. Amid the chaos of the first few months of college, your child will benefit from having some idea of the key people who are in her corner if she needs them.

Check in

Revisit this conversation over the holidays. Is his first year measuring up to his expectations? Why or why not? What might he have done differently? You could even include younger siblings in this conversation, because it could save them many headaches when it's their turn to head off to college.

Locate your mute button

Keep your thoughts to yourself about how you think his college career should be going. This process is about teaching him how to solve his own problems, and how to form a plan and follow it through. If that first year does look like his perfect ideal year, imagine how proud he will be that he made that happen. If you take over, you will turn college into your victory, not his, and once again, this will undermine his sense of autonomy and competence, putting off his eventual emergence into adulthood. He's in a race against time, and in less than four years, he's going to have to go out into the big, bad world and fend for himself. He can't afford to have any of these formative experiences taken away from him.

Roommate issues don't involve you

As we've seen, learning how to deal with people whose ideas, background and habits are different from your own is a great learning opportunity. Once your child has chosen (or been assigned) that roommate, do not call, text, "friend" on Facebook, or Google that roommate. You won't be living with him; your kid will.

Professors don't want parental input

Do not get involved in disputes over grades, seating, or scheduling. Ever. Not if your child is shy, not if your child is failing, and certainly not if your child is too busy to deal with it because she is on spring break. Not only will you be depriving your child of a valuable opportunity to learn how to stand up for herself and reason with other adults in a mature and competent manner, but professors will lose all respect for you and your child.

Kids will ask for help when they need it

Trust that your children will call (or text) when they need you, but it might not be as often as you'd like. Keep in mind that they will call more often if you are not the type of parent to jump straight into an inquiry of grades, assignments, and whether or not your child made that appointment with the economics professor that you asked him to make last week.

These four years will provide the friendships, connections, lessons and experiences that will shape his adult life. Support your child, but know when to step back and allow him to embark on his own life. One of Hartstein's clients, a thirty-year-old woman whose parents have managed every aspect of her life and now finds herself, in Hartstein's words, "unable to live life on life's terms", offers this warning to parents like hers: "You know, too much support isn't a good thing. It doesn't teach you anything, like how to survive in the world. It can be a really huge disservice."

Give your child the opportunity to succeed. Send him

to college with a first aid kit and some emergency cash, and a confidence in all the things he will learn. Let him have the freedom to create the person he wants to be and understand the paths and influences he does not want to follow. If he fails, and he will, that will be evidence of a dead-end experience and he will learn not to go down that road again. If, however, you pave the way out of that dead end, he learns nothing new. You have lived your life and learned the lessons it has granted you. Now it's his turn.

Part III

Succeeding at School: Learning from Failure is a Team Effort

10

PARENT-TEACHER PARTNERSHIPS: HOW OUR FEAR OF FAILURE UNDERMINES EDUCATION

In my teaching life, I correspond with parents all day long, communicating news about late assignments, congratulations for hardwon victories, and updates on behavioural problems. Each time I email or call home, I struggle with the contents of those emails or phone calls, particularly when they contain bad news or criticism, and strive to keep my words gentle and measured, yet firm. I pray I've struck the right tone, and that my communication triggers the start of a great partnership, a concerted effort between parents and educator, working together to accomplish what no one person can do alone. Some go well, and some... well, some don't.

The example I hold up as the epitome of a great home and school partnership occurred one afternoon when a student posted something inappropriate about another student online during school hours. Teachers and administrators researched the incident, figured out who was responsible and contacted parents within hours to let them know we would be instigating appropriate school disciplinary steps in response to their children's actions. The parents thanked us for addressing the issue fairly and quickly, for identifying the guilty parties in the situation and assured us that they would be following up with further discussion at home. Everything went according to plan: we felt supported by the parents, the parents felt supported by the school, and the students understood that home and school were a united front. This outcome is a bestcase scenario, and when it happens, it's a beautiful thing. Everyone benefits from the unified effort, and the students are held accountable and allowed to learn from their mistakes.

However, homeschool communications also have the potential to go poorly, and the resulting conflict can be disastrous for the education of the student concerned. Here's my own sad and humiliating account of just how wrong it can go.

It's 8:11am, and I'm late for my first class. I have to teach seventh-grade Latin, but I'm trapped in my boss's office, an irate parent blocking my exit. The mother doesn't know I am in here; I could wait her out. But maybe, if I can get some momentum and keep my eyes down, I might be able to sneak by her and escape unscathed. I briefly consider climbing out the window, but the ground slopes away from the building and the fall could kill me. I'm willing to risk it, I realise, as I peek out of the crack between the office door and its frame. I check the clock: 8:12. Damn. I take a deep breath, remind myself that my students are waiting for me to teach them how to *amo, amas, amat,* and step out from behind the door. Between my self-imposed prison and freedom lies this angry mother lion, tensed and eager to eviscerate anyone who comes between her cub and a top-tier high school. Unfortunately, I'm her preferred prey today, because I'm the teacher who emailed her thirty minutes ago with news of her son's low grade in English class.

What has brought parents and teachers to this place? How could I, an otherwise confident person, a professional with more than a decade of teaching under my belt, feel compelled to hide from a woman who should be my ally in the quest to educate her child? On the other hand, I can't imagine this mother is having an enjoyable school year, either. All the worry and anxiety over every tiny detail of her son's school day, all the frustration and anger directed at his teachers for their perceived failings and shortcomings... it must be exhausting. She certainly never *looks* happy. In fact, many of my students' parents look positively overwrought and precariously close to their breaking points.

But enough about us. We are merely collateral damage. The real victims in this situation are the students. Many of my students express tension and outright fear for weeks before report cards come out, and in the days before parents' evenings, they look as if they are bound for the gallows. Even when they adore their parents and respect their teachers, loyalty to one gets in the way of the relationship with the other, sort of like negotiating divorcing parents. My students cannot possibly trust me completely when I am locked in battle with their parents.

Despite tensions between parents and teachers, decades of research shows that positive family-school relationships are vital to student success. Positive parent-teacher partnerships don't just benefit students; they are a boon to everyone involved. Teachers who encourage parental involvement in school are rated more favourably than teachers who do not, even in unrelated areas such as educational effectiveness. Students learn more when families are involved in their education, and parents feel more engaged and invested in their child's education when teachers invite them into the process.

If this is the case, why do so many teachers cite the challenge of dealing with their students' parents as their main reason for abandoning the classroom? Educators and education researchers advocate and praise the value of family involvement in education, yet teachers readily admit scepticism about the potential success of that involvement. I'm not the only educator shaking in my boots, even if I am the only one who has been reduced to hiding in a dark office. However, based on hundreds of conversations with teachers and administrators on this subject, maybe I'm not.

A teacher of more than forty years explains the shift in the parent-teacher relationship this way:

When I started teaching, the parent, schools and law enforcement officials were all on the same side. Authority was aligned and united. It was not to be questioned. Then came the '60s and its aftermath. For the children of the '60s, especially those who spent their teens in that era, the relationship between citizen and authority became much less secure. Authority was indeed to be questioned. Differences were to be celebrated and accepted. Eventually, the children of the '60s became parents. Those who questioned authority now became the questioning authority.

What has been lost, first and foremost, is the trust we

192

must have in each other to help children through their mistakes and emerge with an education. Kids need the space to fail, and teachers need the time and benefit of the doubt to let that failure play out in the form of learning. One longtime teacher and administrator from a large state school outlines the opportunities that are lost to teachers when they are barred from the fertile educational territory opened up when their students fail:

> When parents step in to defend a child's poor choice or mistake or failure in order to avoid the "consequence" of that action or performance, they tend to lose sight of the fact that if the student does not have the experience of making mistakes and living and learning with the consequence of that mistake or failure, college may be a very difficult experience thousands of miles away from the security of Mum and Dad when he eventually has to deal with an experience on his own. Mistakes are opportunities to grow. Failures or unsuccessful attempts are the same, and students need to live through those experiences to develop a toolbox of coping mechanisms to lift them and move them forward.

That toolbox, the accumulated store of skills students earn through their failures, adaptations and growth, is more important than any mathematical formula or grammatical rule, and this is why teachers are frustrated when they are not allowed to help students stock up and hone these skills. A mother of three explained her autonomy-supportive strategy this way: "If you knew there was something that could help your child, that could give them 'tools' to help them later in life, could help them face the future with more strength, maturity to face life's challenges, wouldn't you do it?"

So, if you are ready to forge a true partnership with your child's teacher, and to give your child the tools that will help him later in life, here are some guidelines that will help you create positive partnerships with teachers from the very beginning of primary school.

Show up at school with an attitude of optimism and trust

Your child is listening and watching, particularly on the first day of school. If you are trusting and relaxed, he will be trusting and relaxed. If you are nervous and watching for the teacher to screw up, he will be nervous and watch for his teacher to screw up. My best student-teacher relationships have always been with the kids whose parents assume that I will take good care of their child and give him the education he deserves, and the worst were with students whose parents distrusted me from the start. You don't have to love your child's teacher, or disregard negative rumours, but if you give teachers the benefit of the doubt, they will be much more likely to give your child the same.

Be on time

I watched Judd Apatow's film *This Is 40* recently, and was tickled by a scene in which the mother drops her kid off at school, and the teacher greets her at the door with the following exchange:

194

Teacher:
Hi – um, listen, Charlotte really needs to get here on time because she really just needs the extra time to settle in.

Mum:
[mystified] We are on time.

Teacher:
[deadpan] Being on time means being early.

Judd Apatow is absolutely right. Being on time means being early because kids require at least fifteen minutes to wrap their sleepy brains around the fact that they have arrived at school. Younger ones need to check in with friends and stow their lunchboxes, and older kids need to unload their backpacks, hand in work, gather their materials for the day, and mentally prepare for their first class. I've watched students stand in front of their lockers, hair all askew from heavy sleep, for a full five minutes, just staring at their books before they are able to muster the wakefulness required to select their materials. Adolescents are particularly challenged first thing in the morning due to the fact that teens' sleep cycles are plagued by a "phase delay", or delayed melatonin release. Simply put, adolescents get sleepy about two hours later than adults, and consequently, have a tendency to wake up later. Consider how well you would function if you woke up sleep-deprived, then parked your car and ran straight into a presentation to the head of the company with no coffee, no time to take off your coat, no moment to take a deep breath and prepare for the day. Students who rush into school at the last minute remain frazzled for much of the morning.

Students who arrive on time – I mean early – and have an opportunity to take stock of the day are more prepared for class in terms of their materials and their emotional state.

If you take your child to school make sure that lateness doesn't become a habit. Start your day earlier, if you have to. I have been in charge of marking down lateness for the past five years at my school, and I can attest to the fact that kids who are late are inevitably stressed-out, particularly if the lateness is not their fault. Children have a heightened sense of justice, and they understand that being late is unfair and disrespectful to their teachers and to the other kids who are distracted when they arrive late to class or homeroom, so don't heighten their anxiety by allowing blame for being late to fall on their shoulders.

Read the school's attendance policy and follow it

Don't schedule term-time holidays; don't return from summer holidays the day after school starts, or leave the day before terms ends. If you have a genuine reason for your child to miss school, give the teacher as much notice as you can.

Nothing is more frustrating to a teacher than a student who announces he is leaving for a week tomorrow and would like to know what he will have to do to keep up with the class.

Be friendly and polite

We tend to abandon good, old-fashioned friendliness and congeniality when our lives become hectic and overwhelmed. Not only does friendliness make the day flow more easily; it really does make a difference to the way teachers perceive parents and their children. I'd love to say that teachers can mentally separate even the most wonderful children from their surly parents, but it's not always possible. Alice could be my favourite student, the most incredible, charismatic, kind and generous student I have ever taught, but if Alice's mother is abusive or unreasonable, our relationship is tainted. As much as I want to keep Alice separate from her mother, that memory of her mother coming into school and waggling her finger in my face in front of an entire class of students is always there, colouring the way I think about our relationship and my communications with the child. Even if I could banish Alice's mother from my brain and keep the two completely separate, I certainly don't want to voluntarily make contact with someone who humiliated me in front of my students.

Furthermore, when it comes time to bring up concerns – or praise – about Alice, I am going to be reluctant to pick up the phone or send an email if her mother has been rude to me. That's just basic human nature. When the mouse learns it's going to be shocked when it reaches for the tasty treat, you'd better believe that mouse will stop reaching for the tasty treat, even if it's hungry. Freud noted that it's in our basic human nature to "attain pleasure and avoid pain", and humiliation, distrust, passiveaggressive interpersonal communication and disrespect are excruciatingly painful for teachers. Consequently, if you humiliate, distrust, or offer up passive-aggressive communications with your child's teacher, be prepared for radio silence to follow. We will continue to educate your child and hold him to the same standards, but we sure as heck will avoid talking to you about it unless we have to.

197

Project an attitude of respect for education

If your attitude toward teachers is one of respect for the educational process, your child will be a lot more likely to respect, enjoy and engage in her education, and we will look forward to telling you all about it. There's nothing I love more than intercepting a parent at dropoff or pickup just to tell him about a fantastic contribution his daughter made in class that day, or that as I read his daughter's last paper, it occurred to me just how far her writing has come over the past year. Teachers cherish good relationships with parents and take great pleasure in offering up those communications. Teachers are also a lot less likely to be upset by constructive criticism or negative feedback from a parent they have come to like or admire. Some of the most effective feedback I have received about flaws in my teaching has come from parents. However, if that same feedback had come from a parent I don't respect, or a parent who cries wolf every time her son comes home with a complaint, I would be a lot less likely to take that feedback as useful or valid.

Model enthusiasm for learning

Your attitudes toward education will be your child's attitude. Likewise, your enthusiasm for the process of learning for learning's sake is vital to instilling the same in your child. Let your child see you reading for fun. Pick up a book about a topic you know nothing about and become the resident expert on something, maybe Greek gods, Renaissance art, or botany. Learn to play an instrument. Go to the library and browse books in subjects you've never read or check out college courses and take a class in something new. Find out what your child is reading at school and get an audio version of that book for the car. Talk about the book, about the big ideas, and what the characters are up to. You will get the opportunity to understand what your child is reading and learning, which will open the door to conversations about what it would take to make Boo Radley come out, or why Holden Caulfield wears that ridiculous hunting hat.

Make sure your first communication with a teacher is positive

One of my favourite bits of teacher advice applies to parents, and is a great way to ensure a positive relationship from your very first moments with your child's teacher. In his book *The Essential 55*, educator Ron Clark advises teachers to make sure the first interaction they have with parents is positive. This is a great guideline for parents, as well. Make contact in the first month or so of school and find something nice to say. Mention an interesting dinnertime conversation you had with your child about a book he's reading in class. "We had a great conversation last week about that Frost poem you taught Kevin," for example. As long as the feedback is genuine, it will create the beginnings of a productive bond. This sort of communication places parents firmly on the same team as teachers, and sets the stage for trust, even when students flounder or fail.

Invite teacher feedback

Teacher feedback is valuable, so encourage it from day one. Let teachers know that you view both positive and negative observations as a vital part of your child's education and the parent-teacher partnership. On a practical level, let the teacher know how to reach you. If you prefer email, let her know. If you work long hours or the night shift, or would prefer that she call you at work, let her know that, too. Conversely, know how the teacher would like to receive communications and adhere to that preference. When you do reach out, understand that most teachers either cannot or will not be checking email throughout the day. They are supposed to be teaching your children, after all. Ask the teacher whether she'd prefer email or phone, and comply. Make sure the teacher knows you are not just paying lip service to the idea of feedback; let her know that you are ready and willing to listen.

Wait a day before emailing a teacher over a perceived emergency or crisis

While you should absolutely let teachers know about emergencies at home as soon as possible, wait a day to complain about homework, assignments, disciplinary actions, and the like. These may feel like crises in the moment, but if you wait, you may just realise that they are not. Besides, as you should be moving your child toward a greater responsibility for discussing issues with her teachers, these twentyfour hours give you a perfect interval to develop a game plan with your child. Take this time to breathe and calm down. Once you and your child have distance from the emotional side of the incident, take some time to talk about what happened. Ask open-ended questions about what was happening before, during, and after the incident.

Let teachers know about big events unfolding at home

Don't wait until the divorce or child custody battle or chronic nightmares or eating disorder has gotten to a crisis point before filling the teacher in on what's happening at home. If you let your child's teacher in on these things early, it will be much easier to accommodate, adapt and help children cope at school. For many students, school provides a refuge from troubles at home, and the more teachers can create that sense of refuge and safety, the better. Make an appointment to speak with the teacher if you feel a face-to-face is important or if the situation is too sensitive to put down in writing. However you choose to do it, the goal is to communicate with the teacher so she can help your child.

Express interest in what is being taught

Let the teacher know you are interested in what's going on at school, and find ways to explore that learning at home. Find opportunities to ask your child to teach you about something she learned in school. Feign ignorance about why lava forms, or how pulleys work, and allow your child to enlighten you. Ask for details about what is happening at school, and don't accept "I don't remember" as an answer. When parents complained that this was the stock answer they received from my students, I started sending home weekly bullet lists of the big ideas we discuss in class, from daily etymology or cultural literacy lessons to capsule summaries about the authors and stories we read. Once you know a little bit about what's going on at school, you can open the door to conversations about that material and how it relates to the greater world.

Find opportunities to express gratitude

Teachers receive daily complaints, but it's rare to hear feedback about the successes. I'm not suggesting that you invent praise or compliments out of thin air, but when things are going smoothly, or if your child is talking about something she's excited about in school, thank her teacher. Better yet, write a thank you note. I guarantee that note will either get tacked to the wall of the teacher's office or tucked in a special folder she keeps in her desk drawer. I have one of those folders in my desk drawer, and I've carried some of the notes inside it with me since my very first teaching job. The value of a thank you cannot be overstated, and the practice of expressing gratitude is a great lesson to model for your kids.

Begin with the assumption that you have an interest in common – the student

The vast majority of teachers go into education because they care about children and are excited about the subject they teach. What struck me over and over again during interviews with teachers was the genuine concern and love most teachers feel for their students, so keep this in mind when you are tempted to assume that a teacher has it in for your child.

Protect your child's right to fail

Be emotionally prepared for the challenges your child will face in the coming year, particularly as she battles her way through transitions and milestones. She will take her cues from you, so project confidence in her and in your ability to refrain from rescuing her from the challenge of these transitions and milestones. Keep your eyes on the prize of autonomy and competence, and remember that failure is going to be a vital part of her education, as vital as maths or English or science.

To that end, protect her right to fail. Give her the time and space she needs to be disappointed in herself. Finally, encourage her perseverance as she picks herself up, dusts herself off, and learns from experience that she is capable of rebounding from those failures. These guidelines don't change much over the years between the first day of kindergarten and the last day of sixth form. Each and every first day of school offers the promise of a new beginning, a chance to be understood for who we really are, and an opportunity to learn from the mistakes we've made along the way.

Give your child a voice

From the very first day of school, it is vital that children learn to speak up for themselves. One reception class teacher told me, with great frustration, about parents who inform her on the first day that because their child is not yet capable of speaking for himself, she is going to have to "intuit"... "These children are able to do *so* much more than parents are willing to believe, and they can speak for themselves."

From the first day of school, she expects her students to talk to her, and politely asks parents not to speak for their children when they bring them in. She explains that she wants her students to feel heard and understood, and in order to do that, they must be able to communicate with her. Furthermore, she expects her students to talk to each other before seeking her intervention. "They have to spend the time trying things out and messing it up, learning how to make themselves heard, and making mistakes in those communications, or independence won't happen. Kids are not born knowing how to negotiate for themselves, it takes a long time," she said.

As social interactions get more complex with age and maturity, teachers will expect students' ability to communicate to improve along with their ability to reason and think critically. Teachers respect students who are able to stand up for themselves. When your child is dissatisfied with something that has happened at school, whether she is upset about a mark or feels a teacher has acted unfairly, she should always be encouraged to speak to the teacher directly.

If your child feels she is being misunderstood and has been treated unfairly, encourage her to prepare a defense. I tell my students that the skill I respect most is the ability to calm down, think logically about the situation, and then engage in a balanced and rational conversation about conflict. I am always going to be much more willing to change my mind – or a mark, for that matter – if the student approaches me with a reasoned argument for change.

Remember that truth often lies between two perceptions

I trust my children, and yet I am aware that truth is slippery, a subjective and elusive beast. Truth is subject to human frailty and flaws in perception, and this applies to even the most trustworthy and honest children. If you approach your child's teacher or another parent with the assertion that your child is completely free of fault, you are going to lose credibility before you've even begun to advocate for your child. Keep an open mind and hope others will do the same.

After talking with many parents about their child's behaviour at school versus their behaviour at home, it's become clear to me that the child you know at home may not be identical to the child his teachers and other students know at school. This is completely normal and understandable. Friends, academic pressure, chemistry between teacher and student, and a million other factors affect who we are in a given situation. When a teacher reports that something is going on with your child, at least consider that the teacher might be right. Rejecting teacher observations out of hand is a common defensive move, one I have fallen for myself, but it damages relationships and delays the opportunity for academic, psychological or medical help for a student.

If you are concerned with a teacher's actions, talk to that teacher

Resist the temptation to go over the teacher's head to the principal, at least at first. The principal is put in an impossible position when a parent goes to them straight away, because the head is forced to respond in some way, and it's highly unlikely she was present for whatever altercation or conflict took place. Make an appointment to talk to the teacher sooner rather than later, because as time passes, resentments mount, details fall away in memory, and the opportunity to make things right is lost.

The best time to conduct a parent-teacher meeting is at a scheduled meeting

The teacher may look available first thing in the morning at school drop-off, but he's not. He's doing an essential part of his job: helping his students settle into their day and organising his thoughts before the first lesson of the morning. The first and last moments of the day are often the most hectic for teachers, and to have an informed conversation about a student, teachers need time to mentally prepare. Even if the teacher offers to go out in the hall or in her office to talk to you right that minute, don't be tempted. And for the record, cocktail parties, the vegetable aisle of the supermarket, and the doctor's office are not appropriate places to initiate impromptu parent-teacher conferences. All three of these examples are my own, and each was extremely awkward in its own way.

Read the school's handbook and disciplinary policy

Too many parents find out about detentions, or other disciplinary issues after the fact, and it's difficult to talk to your child about actions and consequences when you do not know how the school deals with these issues. If the rules are different at school than they are at home, you have to know that, too. Finally, remember that if you are incensed and upset by a teacher's actions or discipline, talk to the teacher about your concerns and refrain from trashing the teacher in front of your child. It is very confusing for children (particularly young ones) to understand when parents and teachers, their authority figures, collide.

Do not intervene in the school's disciplinary actions unless there has been an egregious misunderstanding or something is unsafe or truly unreasonable. The school's rules may not be your rules, and you might not impose the same disciplinary action, but your child needs to understand that in the real world, people must abide by rules they don't always agree with. Your child needs to own up to the consequences of breaking school rules, rebound from that and move on with her education.

Parenting children through school crises is an emotional, painful process. I have felt out of control, frustrated with teachers, even wanted to retaliate against some other kid in the sandpit who slighted my darling child and threw sand in his face. When I feel that way, I try to remember that I'm being a good parent every time I don't intervene in the hardships he faces in the classroom and on the playground. My child's life is only going to get harder, more emotionally complicated, more frustrating. Those mean teachers will become mean professors and mean bosses and mean neighbours, and if I allow him to sail through his childhood free of frustration and upset, I am setting him up for misery. When the stakes get higher, and the painful episodes get more painful, he's going to know how to be resilient and resourceful without me. Don't save your children. Let them learn as early as prep school how to walk up to someone who has misunderstood or mistreated them, stand up for themselves, and be heard.

Support the student-teacher partnership, even when it's challenging

The relationships children forge with their teachers can become some of the most important of their lives. I don't know anyone who does not have fond, lasting memories of at least one teacher, and when I asked people to share their very best memories of teachers, along with why those teachers meant so much to them, the responses came pouring in.

> Honestly, the hard ones were the best ones, the ones who also seemed to take a personal interest and work with you to help you succeed.
>
> Sister John Andre, my sixth-grade English teacher, was so excited about grammar. She would turn away from the board while diagramming a sentence to literally clap her hands with excitement. That love of learning rubbed off on me, and she was the first person to call me a writer.
>
> Mrs Peters, my high school English teacher. She gave me an F on a quiz, and I never, ever came

to class unprepared again.

My favourite teacher cared about me. It is that simple. He took the time to get to know me, and therefore I felt a strong sense of commitment to him. I knew he cared about me and I would run through a wall for him.

Over the course of a child's education, he is going to have many teachers. Some will be great, some will be adequate, and some will fall short, and your child is going to have to learn to deal with all of them. If he is lucky, one or two of those teachers will be people your child will recall with great fondness, as role models who changed his life. But at some point during your child's education, he will be assigned teachers he doesn't like. There will be teachers he doesn't know how to talk to, teachers who are exceptionally demanding, teachers he doesn't completely understand, and teachers whose expectations are unclear. This, dear parents, is a good thing. These teachers will be the people who will teach your child how to deal with the many challenging, unpleasant, contrary, and demanding people he will encounter over the course of his life. He will have problematic bosses, employees, boyfriends, girlfriends and spouses, your child will have to learn how to get along with all of them. As a parent, I know how painful it can be to witness our children's pain and discomfort when faced with a bad relationship. When my child is in pain, when he's frustrated or disappointed by his attempts to play the game of school according to a teacher's quirky rules, my first instinct is to get defensive, grab my child, and flee the playing field. But that game will go on. The sooner he learns how to adapt, the better prepared he'll be when it's his time to play, no matter what version of the rules is in force.

11

HOMEWORK: HOW TO HELP WITHOUT TAKING OVER

Homework comes in many forms – from practice to preparation, from useless to useful, from engaging to downright tortuous. Whatever form it takes and regardless of where you stand on the topic of homework's purpose and utility, homework is your *child's* job, not yours. *Your* job is to support, encourage and redirect your children when they are young, and as they get older, to make your expectations clear and get out of their way.

Yes, yes, I know; easier said than done. It's easy to stand back and give your child autonomy when homework is a simple maths facts review or when long-term assignments remain safely in the distant future. However, when the whining and the complaints of "But I don't *want* to do homework!" and "It's too hard!" rise to a shriek, it is tempting to take over or simply divulge the correct answers so the torture can end and family members can get on with their lives. Don't succumb. These stressful moments, when your child's frustration levels are high, harbour the most valuable opportunities to foster diligence, perseverance and grit in your child. Kids learn the most about sticking with a task when it's hard, when they are sure they will never figure something out, or when they are suffering the consequences of their own procrastination or botched planning. Even more important, homework that's challenging is more valuable from a learning perspective than easy homework, so stick

Each night he and his wife would spend hours struggling through their eight and ten-year-old daughter's homework assignments. The parent would stay present for when a child became stuck, feeding a self-fulfilling cycle of dependency.

to your guns. Be strong. When that poster for the science fair looks like a glue-smeared mess, and it's an hour past bedtime, that's precisely when you should step back and walk away.

It may seem harmless to step in, but the damage is cumulative. Every time you take over, and rescue your child from working out a challenging maths problem or thesis statement on her own, you undermine your child's sense of confidence and autonomy. Completing the task herself is its own incentive, a reward infinitely more important than test scores. Think long-term goals. When tonight's stressful homework assignment has been forgotten, she may not even remember that poster, or the specific maths problem that tripped her up, or the thesis statement she could not get just right. What she will retain, however, are the long-term benefits she gains when she unravels that maths problem on her own or perseveres with the science experiment until she reaches a conclusion all on her own. She may also feel disappointed in her efforts or her abilities or embarrassed the next day when she faces her teacher and her class with an incorrect answer, but these are her lessons to learn. Your job is not to save her from disappointment or embarrassment, but to sympathise, support, and help her find the strength and skills she will need for tomorrow night's task. Let her find what this student found when she did battle both with maths, and her better angels, in the middle of the night:

> One night when I was working on the last problem on a particularly hard maths assignment, I had the thought, "What if I stopped working on this last proof? What if I gave up?" I knew I could do the work, but it would take a long time and I did not want to do that. I thought about it for a long while. I actually packed up my schoolbooks and went to bed, only to be awakened hours later by the drive to finish. I got up at about one in the morning and I finished that proof. Despite the resulting fatigue, I felt good. I knew that I had done my best. I had not felt that good about myself and my school work for a long time.

Whenever any child is taking a long time to complete her work, or complaining that she simply can't get everything done, I suggest that parents run through this quick checklist before rushing to her teacher to complain.

- Check vision and hearing. Vision and hearing impairments can be the cause of comprehension dips and changes in performance, a cause that's easy to miss unless schools conduct regular screenings.

- Make sure your child is getting enough sleep. Preschoolers need 11–13 hours, children from age five to ten need 10–11 hours, and teens need somewhere between 8.5 and 9.25 hours of sleep a night; less than that wreaks havoc on concentration, memory, learning, attention, executive functioning and behaviour.
- Gauge challenge. If you believe your child really can't manage the work she is being given, talk to the teacher. Conversely, if the work is too easy, that is equally problematic. Research shows that children lose focus and interest when tasks are too simple and, therefore, not engaging. That magical "flow" of losing oneself in a task happens only when a task is challenging. Challenge and desirable difficulties trigger encoding, and if the student persists, mastery.

Once you've turned an objective eye to your child's vision, hearing, sleep and level of challenge, look at *how* your child is doing that homework. When I hear from parents that a student is spending hours and hours on homework, I like to quietly and surreptitiously watch that student when I have assigned an independent task in class. Some students look as if they are working, but when I pay close attention, I can see that they actually waste a lot of time, skipping around from task to task, stopping and starting, doodling – and that's without access to a computer, smartphone, or any other obvious distraction. Other students, who get down to work on an assignment, work straight through, check it off their list, and move on, get two or three times as much work done as the students who mess around. Often the parents of the students who waste time mention the huge homework load their children deal with at night, and we point out that much of their homework could be accomplished during study periods, that the students who take advantage of these periods take home much less homework than the students who do not. If homework seems excessive, try this exercise at home. Watch your child when he does his homework, and take note of when real work is getting done and when he is fiddling and fooling around with other stuff. Once you've taken an objective look at the accumulated time of "real work" your child is doing, and the amount still seems excessive, then, by all means, figure out which subjects are the biggest offenders and talk to those teachers about their homework load.

If teachers claim your child is in the minority, and homework takes a reasonable amount of time for others in the class, ask the teacher how long the homework is meant to take and then try the Timer Cure. Credit for the Timer Cure goes to Alison Gorman, a maths teacher who noticed that some students were taking a long time to do problem sets at home, but in school, where there are no distractions and a set time limit, those same students managed to finish the entire assignment, often with time to spare.

The Timer Cure works like this: remove all distractions and set the time for the length of time the teacher has recommended. Make sure your child can see the timer so that he knows when time is running out. Remind him that he can't spend a half hour on one problem and expect to finish the entire problem set in the time allotted, so he is going to have to budget his time. Nine times out of ten, the student will meet the clock.

Now for the practical details: when you should help and what that help should look like, when is it time to back off, and how to help children find the silver lining around their homework failures. The key is to stay focused on the goal of your child's autonomy.

Here are some practical steps you can take to help children of all ages learn how to organise, strategise and take responsibility for their homework. For young children, parents will need to teach these steps at first, in order to form good habits, but over time, you should expect your child to take ownership of these tasks. If your child is older and she has never had to step up and take charge of her own learning, giving her control over these first steps can be an ideal place to start:

- Fuel up. Our brains can't work well unless we are nourished and hydrated. Prepare, or encourage your child to prepare a healthy snack and drink of water in order to top off the energy his brain needs to be alert and awake for the work ahead.

- Get rid of distractions. Even small distractions, such as switching between tasks, or a momentary lapse in concentration can lead to mistakes. A recent study showed that even a three-second distraction can double the number of mistakes people make on tasks, probably because the distraction caused the details of those tasks to slip out of short-term memory. Find a quiet, distraction free space for homework time.

- Understand expectations. Know what teachers expect from your child. Many teachers send home or publish weekly plans online to keep parents informed about assignments, so use those to clarify expectations and plan ahead for the rest of the week. If your child is not clear on expectations, encourage them to follow up with their teachers at school.

- Organise and strategise. In study halls, I have students

write a checklist on the whiteboard in the front of my classroom so they are all held accountable for what they need to do. This also allows for reminders from classmates not to forget about maths or French homework. At home, you could ask, "What about English? Isn't Monday grammar day?" and help your child prioritise.

- Suggest your child do the hardest work first. Research shows that self-control is a limited commodity in the human brain, and reserves are likely to be at their highest levels at the start of homework time.

- Evaluate the end product. Teach kids to pause at the end of an assignment, and evaluate if the assignment has been completed according to instructions. Some teachers ask parents to sign off on homework, but move kids in the direction of being able to evaluate on their own whether or not their work meets expectations. Once children are able to do this, inform the teacher that you will no longer be signing off on their work, that the child is responsible for signing off on it themselves.

- Complete what can be completed. If, after repeated attempts, your child cannot complete all of the work, encourage her to break the assignment down and do what she can. Here is where it's important to speak with school teachers about expectations. Some teachers would like parents to talk the child through the work, and others prefer that the sections that the child could not complete be left blank so that the teacher can see what the child does or does not know. My personal preference is that the child do *something* even if he or she can't complete the entire task. In a challenging Latin translation, for example, I ask students to look up the words and list their definitions, or label the parts of speech of the words, even if they can't figure out the precise English translation. The more evidence I have of where the student is going wrong, the more I am able to help get the student back on track.

- Aim for learning, not for perfection. Try to keep the focus on what's really important about homework. Homework is not only about finding the right answers; it's about giving kids the opportunity to practise and expand skills they learned today and to prepare for the skills they will learn tomorrow.

Support, encourage and redirect

When children are young, your job during homework time is to be nearby, busy with other activities. You are present, but not hovering. Supportive, but not intrusive. I often prepare dinner while my younger son does his homework at the kitchen counter. That way, I'm there if he needs support, encouragement or redirection, but I'm busy and won't be tempted to intervene every time he hesitates or makes his attention-seeking moans of frustration. Until he was nine or ten, I checked in on his progress every ten minutes or so, just to make sure he was on track, but now that he's able to identify when he's really stuck, as opposed to momentarily hung up on a concept or instruction, he asks me for help as needed.

It's really important that kids know we have other things to do in our lives than sit next to them and wait for them to get stuck and ask questions. I've spoken with many parents who admit this is how homework happens every night in their homes. One mother, whose children are six and nine, told me, "We sit down as a family at homework time so my husband and I can both be there to help them when they get stuck." Another parent, when we sat down together to problem-solve the nightly tantrums and anxiety attacks his children were having at homework time, painted a similar picture. Each night he and his wife would spend hours struggling through their eight and ten year old daughters' homework assignments. In both cases, the parents would stay present for *when* a child became stuck, feeding a self-fulfilling cycle of dependency.

Some parenting books advise that kids should do homework first, then have the freedom to play as a reward, while other books recommend that kids have the "reward" first, so they are not rushing through homework in order to get to the reward as quickly as possible. Let me propose a novel concept: ask your child where and when she would like to complete her homework. If homework time is a nightly battle, ask the question she may be yearning to answer: "How would *you* like to complete your homework?" Every child is different. Some need time after school to run around and vent some pent-up energy and heebie-jeebies, and others like to get straight down to business and get homework out of the way. Author and parenting expert Vicki Hoefle tells a story in her book *Duct-Tape Parenting* about the nightly battles she and her husband used to fight with their then seven-year-old daughter. Vicki and her husband wanted their daughter to do her homework, and she flat out refused to comply. Finally, in Vicki's words, "it clicked":

The next morning, at breakfast, I asked her the magic question.

"K, in a perfect world, on a perfect day, how would you take care of your homework?" She did not hesitate. She had been waiting for us to listen to her.

"I would get up at 4:30am and do it. I can't do it at night. My brain just won't do it."

"Okay," I said. "How about for the next week, you do your homework whenever you like. Your dad and I will not get in your way. Here's the thing, though. We have to leave the house at 7:15am. No exceptions. Can do you that?"

She thought for maybe ten seconds and then said, "YES."

Vicki and her husband were prepared for this plan to fail, but it did not. Not only did their daughter set her alarm clock and get up the next morning to do her homework; she continues to be an early riser and, according to Vicki, continued to do her homework at four thirty in the morning throughout college.

Once your child has selected a time and place of his choosing, give him time and space to struggle. Make it clear that you are nearby, taking care of your own responsibilities, while he takes care of his. If you have been helping with homework up until this point, this change is going to be a real challenge, but like those toddler temper tantrums that required you to stick to your guns until the battle passed, the homework temper tantrum will end as well, and your student will be more independent and confident for your efforts.

While studies on homework effectiveness in children reveal that homework at primary school has little academic value, there are non-academic benefits to be gained from the nightly task of homework. The ability to initiate, delay gratification, see a task through to completion, and persist through frustration and challenge are incredibly important executive function skills, and homework encourages their development.

While research shows that there is little or no evidence linking primary school homework and achievement, I can support one benefit of homework: it gives teachers feedback on how students are doing in terms of their progress toward mastery. When parents step in and "help", however, teachers get an inaccurate representation of that mastery. One maths teacher told me the story of a thirteen-year-old student whose parents "helped" so regularly and extensively with his homework that while his answers were always correct in his notebook, the work often contained advanced maths concepts, ideas the student was rarely able to explain to the teacher or class when he copied his work on the board. This teacher lamented that she was never really sure where his level of mastery fell, but she quipped that it must be "somewhere between his brilliant and suspiciously above-grade-level homework and his incomplete and below average work in class."

As children get better at taking responsibility for homework, and sticking with it even as the going gets hard, they can begin to experience the real rewards of their persistence: pride and confidence. Kay Wills Wyma recounts the following story about her daughter Snopes in her book *Cleaning House: A Mom's 12-Month Experiment to Rid Her Home of Youth Entitlement.*

Once, when Snopes asked for help on an English paper, I couldn't stop myself from progressively increasing my involvement. I tried to guide her in coming up with descriptive language, but it took too long. I didn't have time to weather stammering and searching for words. Screaming siblings were vying for my attention. So rather than stand behind her, let her type (as slow as that might be), encourage her to struggle through word choices, and make her correct the errors, I literally pushed her aside and took over the helm in front of the computer. I corrected every grammatical error, filled in missing details, and added creativity to pull the reader into her story. Her report on *Redwall* emerged from its cocoon a beautiful butterfly, a far cry from the hairy caterpillar she had shown me moments earlier.

When she came home from school with the paper that not only sported a huge "97" in glaring red marker (firework marks exploding around the number) but also a note from the teacher on how proud she was of the terrific effort, Snopes looked embarrassed, not proud. It wasn't her work being praised, and she knew it.

Snopes lost out on more than genuine, earned praise. She missed out on all those desirable difficulties that would have really solidified the skills she was supposed to be learning as she completed the assignment. Consider the classic example of parental over-involvement: the science fair project. If there's one arena where failure is most desirable and productive, it's in the process of scientific enquiry. Even if the science project is a grand failure, even if the hypothesis is flat out wrong, that's a good thing. In science, negative results are not failures, they are useful data.

As you support your children through their nightly homework efforts, keep their need for desirable difficulties at the top of your list of parenting priorities. When frustrated, kids gripe, whine, wail that they are hopelessly stuck, and otherwise give up, hoping you will intervene and save them. In these moments, resist the temptation to do so. Psychologist, author, and school counsellor Michael Thompson suggests that children's struggles become more manageable when we support their efforts to work through it. "Children need us to recognise their struggle and pay attention to it. That doesn't mean intervene immediately, or to start yelling or panicking, or to come to a premature conclusion." As you recognise and empathise, remain autonomy-supportive and support by redirecting your child's focus and effort. If he is really stuck, give him a new way to think about the problem, but do not step in to solve the problem for him.

Of course, there's a fine line between struggles that promote learning and struggles that inhibit learning and intrinsic motivation. First-year Latin students can't translate *The Aeneid*, and asking them to do so would not result in learning but frustration and anger. Just as we learn the difference between cries that indicate our child is really hurt versus the cries that signal momentary frustration or a call for attention, we need to learn how to hear pleas for homework help that indicate insurmountable difficulties as opposed to transitory, desirable challenges. This is no easy task, and a constantly moving target. Young children have diverse and ever-changing skills and needs, and some children are more independent than others. As their idiosyncratic cognitive and emotional talents and deficits emerge, your role will ebb and flow with their needs. Your role in homework won't be the same in first year as it is in fifth year, but keep your eye on the future. You are there to help your children become independent and rely on their developing skills.

Finally, when the homework session is at an end, remember the lessons of Carol Dweck and the growth mindset. Praise your child for the effort he put into his assignments, particularly when he encountered those frustrating difficulties that pushed him to the limits of what he thought he could do. Make sure he knows that you value his persistence as much as, if not more than, you value the answers he wrote after each problem. Whenever possible, reiterate the concept that the harder we work, and the more we stretch our brains, the smarter we become.

Clear expectations and room to learn

Once your child's executive function skills have started to kick in, it's time to remove yourself from your child's homework duties. Around the beginning of secondary school, research shows that homework begins to have an academic benefit. Quality homework shores up knowledge that has already been encoded, and pushes students to apply that knowledge to new contexts. This final aspect of learning, in which students create answers rather than merely recalling them, is called *generative learning*. Homework that promotes generative learning offers students opportunities to play with skills, exercise some trial and error, and create their own answers. While generative learning is vital to mastery, it is also *hard*. Generative learning does not come easily, and when this valuable and precious kind of learning is going on, expect to see some blood, sweat and tears. It won't look like primary school homework, in which answers fit tidily in squares pre-printed on maths worksheets. Generative learning, when done right, should travel outside the lines, disregard boundaries of subject matter, and stretch students' abilities to the limit.

I had the opportunity to witness a particularly messy display of generative learning recently when I served as a practice judge for a FIRST Lego League team. FIRST Lego League is an educational robotics program in which teams of kids invent a solution to some problem they have identified out there in the world. When it came time for the students to run through their presentations, I squirmed in my seat and held my tongue as the students tried, and failed, and tried again to communicate solutions to the problems they had identified. It was all I could do to keep from holding my head in my hands as their prototypes failed to work as planned and they argued about last-minute improvisations. I was anxious about how they would fare in the real competition the next day, as these prototypes were clearly not ready to be deployed in the real world, let alone in front of a panel of judges. The next day, I received an email from the team's parent supervisor to thank me for my help and to announce that the kids had received an award for their work. Specifically, they were honoured for the way they approached the challenge they were given and for the manner in which they embodied the FIRST Lego League core values. Notably, the core values state, "What we discover is more important than what we win." All of that failure, failure that nearly gave me an ulcer, resulted in a great learning experience for the students.

In order to take advantage of the more complex generative learning assignments kids face in secondary school, some students may continue to need guidance with long-term planning and time management. However, these maturing students should be maintaining their own plan book or calendar and beginning to take responsibility for their work and deadlines. Unless they want to talk through an assignment or get your feedback on an idea, parents should not be involved in homework at all.

Think back to your childhood, to those days when you simply felt ready for the school day, when you had worked hard on your homework and felt *really* confident and prepared. Remember those mornings walking to school or riding the bus, when you could not wait for the day to start because you were not just willing to be called on, but eager to show off what you'd accomplished the night before? Keep that feeling in mind when you are tempted to take over your child's homework. Don't deprive her of those feelings of competence. Let her experience both her failures and her successes, and let her take ownership and pride in her work and abilities. You can cheer her on as she progresses, but you can't sit next to her at the dining-room table and hold her hand forever. This is her journey, her personal quest to slay her dragons and secure her just rewards.

12

THE REAL VALUE OF A LOW MARK

I received an email last year from Maggie, a worried and desperate mother who wrote to ask my advice about her son, John, who was about to be kicked out of his academically selective school due to his failing grades. As the other schools in the area were dreadful (so dreadful that the principal and many of the teachers had just been fired), she was desperate to keep him enrolled at his current school. A meeting had been set for the following morning with John's teachers to decide his future:

I admit that I am guilty of all sorts of over-parenting crimes, like catering to my kids for picky eating, or bringing my son his lunch if he forgets it. His shelves are lined with trophies and he has several medals for perfect FCAT scores and Math Meet competitions. He has never had to study or barely lift a finger in order to achieve high marks or win his school's PRIDE award (highest mark). Gifted school is making him work like he has never had to in his life and he's been failing his strongest subjects, maths and languages. I think I have done all I can without actually following him to class and listening in. I nag, and push, and keep my fingers crossed. Now that John has received these failing grades, and the consequences might just be expulsion, he claims that he really wants to stay at his current school. He has never expressed actually wanting to go to school – any school, so I think this is a good sign.

I suggested the following plan to Maggie: first, she should sit down for a serious talk with John in order to figure out whether or not he is truly dedicated to keeping his place in his current school. I told her to be honest, to explain how dire the situation has become, and describe his other school options in the district. Finally, she should tell him she has a plan, but only if he is truly willing to do what it takes to reclaim his spot at the gifted and talented school.

If John says yes, that he is ready and willing to do what it takes to stay in his current school, then it's time to reveal Maggie's new expectations for John.

- School, and all it entails, will be John's responsibility, the homework, organisation, planning, all of it.
- Maggie will not nag, remind, cajole, or otherwise interfere in his efforts to succeed.

John agreed to these new expectations, and they shook on it. The next day, Maggie met with John's teachers, described his newfound drive to earn his place at the school, and made the case for a probationary semester, three more months for John to prove himself and his commitment. John's teachers, sensing her desperation, granted her wish. Maggie promised to keep in touch, and my three-month wait for news began.

In my experience, even parents who are enthusiastic about promoting autonomy in their kids get nervous and start second-guessing themselves when actual failing grades are at stake. Even the most stalwart, autonomy-supportive parents can be tempted to fall back on controlling and directive behaviours when poor results marr their child's record. However, these D's, and yes, even those ugly, frightening F's, can prompt a child to step up, take charge, and find his drive. These failing moments are, more often than not, metaphorical roads diverging in a yellow wood, chances for children to decide what's important to them, and whether or not they want to invest in their own learning.

I'm going to point out the gigantic elephant standing in the middle of this chapter right away. Grades. There's no way around this unfortunate reality, so I'm just going to face it head-on. Grades are extrinsic rewards for academic performance. Extrinsic rewards undermine motivation and long-term learning. Ergo, grades undermine motivation and long-term learning. There. Elephant identified. I'd love to remove the elephant from the room altogether and replace it with something less unwieldy and more attractive, but in most of the world the system of education is currently based on the exchange of grades for performance. I have no choice but to talk about how to retrain our brains and our children to look past the beast and see the other, more meaningful rewards that grades obscure.

Over the years, my students have often shared their feelings about grades and the impact they have on learning and motivation with me. Their collective frustrations are beautifully summed up in an essay written by one of those students:

> In the first years of primary school, when scores and percentages did not matter, I wrote freely and honestly about what made me happy. But then foreign numbers began appearing on my papers, numbers representing other people's approval or disdain. At first those numbers were inconvenient little shapes that hindered my ability to write without care. But soon I began to rely on those numbers. I became addicted to A's, craving more when I got snatches of praise. And I started to drift away from what I had been writing as a younger child. Before I realised it, I was writing for those little, crawling black shapes and red marks.

Students are not the only ones acknowledging the detrimental effect of grading. Teachers are increasingly writing and talking about the harm grading does to their students' learning and the fragile student-teacher bond. English teacher K. C. Potts repeats some version of the following speech to his students at the beginning of each school year:

> I will say many times that grades are the worst thing that ever happened to learning, and until you find a way to establish a healthy relationship with them, they will torment and frustrate you, have you worried and stressed-out, will make you sometimes feel not so good about yourself. Of course, you are better at some things than you are at others. One of education's tasks is to help you recognise your strengths and weaknesses. Try to avoid the compare game whereby you judge your performance by comparing it to

that of others. Doing so is both inevitable and counterproductive. The issue is not what others can do but what you can do.

Many of you aspire to high grades because you see them as a ticket to the college of your choice. And yes, grades do matter. But are they an indication of what you can do? The better motivation: learning how to do something well. Getting an "A" measures that the student "knows how to play the game of school." It does NOT always, as practiced, demonstrate real mastery of material.

Even parents admit that grades get in the way of their relationships with their children. "I never thought I'd be this kind of mum, but here I am. Grades are stressing me out. I think about my kids' grades all the time, every day. I know it's wrong, and it's stupid, and I know the kids get mad at me when I do it, but I can't help it, and these days, I feel like it's all I talk about with them."

Even in the early days of grading, teachers and administrators were dubious as to their utility in measuring learning and mastery. The president of Yale, Rev. Timothy Dwight V, expressed his concerns about the imperfections of the emerging examination and grading system in 1898:

> There are, to say the least, two or three very marked evils and imperfections in the system. One of them has already been hinted at – the impersonality, if the expression may be allowed, which is inseparably connected with them; that is to say, the necessary absence of personal communication between the mind of the examiner and the mind of the one who is examined.

Given the long-standing discontent with our system of

grading, it's odd that test scores and grades have gained such power in education. We talk about them every time our kid walks through the door at the end of the day ("How did you do on that French test?"). Some schools use modern software platforms which give parents the ability to check in on grades 24/7 from the comfort of their homes. Ultimately we have to share them with colleges and hope they are good enough to invite admission.

Teachers, parents and students rely on them and hate them at the same time, and, as we have seen, there's plenty of evidence to show that grades are just about the worst way to promote learning through intrinsic motivation. Researchers asked a group of fifth graders to read a passage from a textbook. It was one of those classic samples given on standardised tests, something that's not very interesting and requires paying attention. One third of the kids were told to read the passage and nothing else, the second third were told they would be tested on their comprehension for a grade, and the final third were told that they would be tested but would not receive a grade. Everyone was tested in the end. The two groups who had no expectation of a grade did better on the test than the kids who knew they were going to be graded. Furthermore, they were more interested and curious about the reading. In another study conducted in Japan, a researcher gave secondary school students weekly maths quizzes. He told half the class that the grades would not count, that the quizzes were just to monitor their learning and progress. The other half were told that the quizzes would impact their final grade. Again, the kids who were not concerned about the impact on their final grades learned more and had higher levels of interest and curiosity. These differences endured over time, too. When the researchers returned at a later date to test these same kids again, the ones who had no expectation of being evaluated retained more of the material than the students who read with the fact that they would be graded in mind

———————————

Grades are an annoying and exhausting fact of life, and despite debate over more effective alternatives, they are not going away any time soon. But there are ways to promote intrinsic motivation and long-term learning in spite of them:

Keep grades in perspective

Grades are not a measure of our children's worth, and often they are not even an accurate measure of their ability. Teachers know this, but even we fall into the trap of equating our students with their grades. While grades *can* be a measure of ability, more often they are a measure of the skills that make for successful students: solid executive function skills, compliance, willingness to please, ability to follow directions, and self-discipline. When I listen to students as they debate the merit of grades, it's clear that kids understand this reality. If you catch an honest and forthcoming teacher at the right moment, she may even reveal that she knows it, too. Grades, for all the weight they carry in our culture, are less important than learning. Learning is the key to understanding our world, and the universe beyond; to communicating with other people, and to innovating for the future of our society. Grades are the key to certain academic institutions and a few office doors. I'd prefer my children and my students to value the former rather than the latter.

If that's not incentive enough, consider this: your child might just want to spend more time with you if you lay off the topic of grades. At an induction event at a local school, a parent asked a student on a panel, "What's the piece of advice you'd give us parents about how to help our kids have a great first year?" Her answer:

> I'd say, give your kids some space and don't always talk about school and grades and stuff. Be there, and talk to them, like at dinner and in the car, but talk about the things they want to talk about. My family eats dinner together every night, and I really want to be around my parents and talk to them, but not about school or grades, just about my life and what's going on. When they just talk about grades, it makes me not want to be around them, and it makes me feel like that's all they care about.

As my sons get older, and I compete with their friends, with technology and all the other diversions in their lives for attention and conversation, I find this advice heartening. If all I have to do is lay off the topic of grades in order to warrant more time and attention, I'm in.

Emphasise goals rather than grades

One way to help kids gain control of their education is to shift your family's focus off grades and on to goals. Because goals are self-determined rather than teacher-determined, they can be a much more useful measurement of success. When kids establish their own goals for learning, they gain a sense of ownership and competence. Earning high marks can provide a temporary high, particularly when a kid has worked hard, but achieving a specific and self-determined goal always transcends the rush of a straight-A report card.

Goals can be a great way to motivate and maintain engagement in school, but in order to be effective, the goals must belong to your child. No matter how small or how nonsensical your child's goals may seem to you, they are his goals, and you should respect that. Even non-academic, seemingly frivolous goals are important, because the process of setting goals is not about the goal itself, but the grit required to put a name to an ambition and see it through to fruition. Simply taking the time to talk about the things they want to achieve over time shows kids that we respect their needs and aspirations.

As your family sets their goals, work on your own. Any time you feel yourself taking over or offering too much advice, go into the other room for a drink of water or excuse yourself to use the bathroom. Take a few deep breaths, and remind yourself of the goal here: autonomy over self-directed goals leads to intrinsic motivation, which leads to better learning and life success. And then breathe.

But in between those breaths, don't forget to praise effort, diligence and perseverance. "I'm so proud of you for keeping yourself organised this week and getting your papers put away. I know that's a tedious job, but you really stuck with it." A common refrain in our house has been "I'm really impressed with how hard you are working on your goal of keeping your room clean," and "It must be nice to be able to do your drawing on a clean desk."

Seek feedback rather than scores

While scores and grades prioritise grades over learning, there is one aspect of modern report cards that is actually quite helpful, particularly when done well. Narrative comments and feedback on students' performance, according to research, are "better than grades at both promoting kids' self-motivation to learn and boosting their achievement." Primary school teachers do a good job of providing feedback in reports, but as soon as grades take over from narrative comments as the main method of evaluation, students and parents begin to lose out. When teachers offer information such as "You did a great job of planning your ideas for this paper, and formulating your thesis, but your body paragraphs don't address the question raised by the thesis," in response to a rough draft of a paper, the student has information that praises the positive elements of her work, addresses failures, and gives useful information she can use to improve performance. In this way, informational feedback works much like praise for effort, and similarly boosts intrinsic motivation, enthusiasm for the task, and later performance. Grades are much less useful. If your child isn't getting this helpful kind of feedback do talk to the teacher and explain why you value it.

Let kids steer their own course

Another opportunity to give kids autonomy and control over their learning is in course selection. As soon as your child has a choice about what classes to take, usually at the point of choosing GCSEs, remember that course selection should be his job, not yours. When he sits down with the

235

high-school course catalogue and prioritises language and music and maths selections, he begins to form expectations and goals for himself in his own mind. Choice is one of the most important aspects of establishing autonomy, and if kids have a say in which classes they take, at what time, and with which teachers, they will have so much more ownership over their education.

Yes, I know you want your child to get into a good university and to take a balance of classes designed to thrill those university admissions tutors. However, which would you prefer: a child who is excited because she has ownership over her education and therefore works hard to reach her own goals, or a disengaged child who feels as if his educational path is not his own? That first kid is going to do better in school, report more happiness in her educational experience, and be much more likely to meet the goals she's created for herself. You can have total control over your child's every move, or you can have an intrinsically motivated kid, but you can't have both.

As you watch your child work toward her goals, make sure she hears that your definition of success includes perseverance in the face of failure. I'd much rather teach a kid who takes risks in his education, even when those risks fail to bear fruit in the end. Students who are too afraid to fail tend to produce boring, uncreative and mediocre work. I try to push those students to take risks, be unconventional in their thinking, and approach the assignment as if they were not being graded.

Find alternative decorations for the fridge

As you shift your family's thinking away from grades and

toward goals and learning, try not to deify report cards as the be-all-and-end-all arbiter of accomplishment. It might be tempting to post that straight-A report card on the refrigerator, but doing so conveys the message that you love your children for their grades, not for themselves. What do you plan to do with "bad" report cards, papers, and tests, if you don't post those on the refrigerator as well? The message is clear to your child when you gush over high grades with "Oh! I'm so proud of you! You are so smart!" and frown over C's. A better way to approach grades is to talk to kids about what went well with a particular assignment or class when they receive a high grade. Ask what approaches worked for your child as he prepared for that French test, and what approaches did not work as well. If he gets a low grade on a test, ask what he might do differently next time, strategies that were successful or problematic. Grades should be a measure of progress, not a destination, so give them the weight and attention they deserve, no more.

Reinforce failure as opportunity

When students admit to me that they are scared to death of failing, I can sympathise.

Of course they are afraid of failure. Most students are. They have been told that to fail is to shatter dreams of college, employment, and ultimately, happiness. I am absolutely aware of the stakes faced in university admissions today, but I still maintain that learning for learning's sake, and the opportunity to establish intrinsic motivation early in a child's education, far, far outweigh the impact of a few low marks, and in fact those low grades are necessary and beneficial lessons. However, how a child reacts and adapts to failures can mean the difference between soul-crushing despair and the impetus to step up his game. All of the research, interviews, and anecdotes I've read about successful people and their failures reveals that people who don't identify themselves as failures just because they have failed, who face their failures head-on and look for lessons in the mistakes, are the ones who emerge triumphant. Those who equate failures with being a failure, who go into denial, or seek to blame others for their failures are doomed to repeat their mistakes over and over again, gaining nothing from the experience. Ken Bain, author of the book *What the Best College Teachers Do*, uses the term "contingent self-worth" to describe the attitude of people who see themselves as failures, when they fail at something:

> If you have a sense of contingent self-worth, if your attitude toward yourself depends on whether you "succeed" or "fail", in a certain domain in comparison with other people, you may stop trying. Subconsciously you decide that the best way to avoid losing is to stay out of the game.

Teach your children to face failure and accept it as valuable feedback. Let them see you taking risks and failing, and talk about those failures as opportunities to better yourself. Tim Harford, author of the book, *Adapt: Why Success Always Starts with Failure*, puts this approach simply: "Biologists have a word for the way in which solutions emerge from failure: evolution." When viewed in that light, the proper reaction to failure is not to deny that it exists, or to kill the messenger, but to evolve in response.

———————————

Three months later, Maggie emailed back to thank me for my advice and fill me in on John's progress. As per their agreement, Maggie stopped nagging and interfering and gave John the reins to his education. She successfully lobbied John's school for a probationary period of one semester. The result? Maggie stepped back, and as she did, John stepped up. Maggie wrote,

> I think John really needed that bad year to learn how to study and do things for himself, rather than to be accustomed to everything being done for him. I don't even have to prompt him to work, which I was fully prepared to do. He does it all on his own. Until now, it's been a total struggle for him to prove his answers and show his work. This year he's finally getting it right.
>
> I'm glad he had his "fail" time at an earlier point rather than later. We all have to face it at some point in our lives, and I think he now understands what he's capable of.
>
> So far so good!

At the end of the school year, John was nominated for the school's "Turnaround Student" award, and he continues to impress his teachers with his drive and determination. John's struggle was not, at its essence, about results. Sure, those failing grades precipitated his transformation, but failing grades were merely a by-product of John's inability to be responsible for his learning. Now that Maggie has agreed to step back, she's no longer his to do list, alarm clock, chef, chauffeur and tutor. She's simply his mother.

Like most kids, John takes his cues from his parents. Your attitude about autonomy and grades will inform your child's attitude. It's that simple. He spends his days immersed in academic competition with his peers, fully aware of the importance of grades, so why not be the one person in his life who doesn't fuel the raging fire of academic pressure and insecurity? I'd much rather be the person my kid wants to talk to over dinner about that funny thing that happened to his friend after maths class, the movie he wants to see next weekend, his hopes and dreams. We have such a limited amount of time with our children as it is, so we might as well enjoy it while it lasts. My favourite view on the value of failing in school comes from long-time teacher Jonathan Shea, who has seen the pattern of try, fail, and try again play itself out over and over:

> Students recover. People do it all the time. And the failure helps them learn about themselves. First, they learn that people want them to be okay. Second, they learn that they can overcome a problem, but that work and attention are more important than genius or perfection. Students need to fail, because this is when they learn to succeed.

Conclusion:

WHAT I'VE LEARNED FROM LETTING GO

I love a good parable; I am an English teacher, after all. My life is spent in pursuit of the stories that can help my students connect their individual journeys to the larger experience of being human. When we read the story of Pip's departure from home and return to redemption in *Great Expectations*, for example, Dickens reveals one potential path through childhood, a route for rectifying our own mistakes and a glimpse of a possible ending. Pip, like us, is imperfect, so it's reassuring to know that he finds his way through the mist and the danger and heartbreak of growing up.

All this imperfection is rendered more tolerable when couched in fiction, or fixed safely in the distant past. Our history textbooks are full of these stories, some accurate, some apocryphal, all of them meant to shore up our identity as a culture based on a tradition of boot-strapping, invention from necessity and the great comeback. The oft-cited story of Edison's education in ten thousand failed lightbulbs, for example, has become one of the most famous stories of failure-turned-success in American history. Edison is quoted, misquoted, and paraphrased all over the internet regarding the lessons of those ten thousand failed lightbulbs and the triumph of that one successful attempt. Google "famous failures", and you'll find an entire day's reading, from the well-worn (Steve Jobs, J. K. Rowling, and Albert Einstein) to the obscure (Alan Hinkes, S. A. Andrée, Akio Morita).

We reprint and repeat these tales of failure because we know they end well. They may contain plot twists and surprise endings, but before we even begin reading, we can bet hard money on the outcome. Against all odds, the invention will work, the championship game will be won, and the astronauts will make it back to Earth. We don't share these stories for their surprise endings, but to remind us that our own mistakes might just be worthwhile in the end. We need to know that our suffering, humiliation, and pain will prove valuable in the final accounting.

If the unpredictability of our own journey is frustrating, the suspense that parents experience as we watch our children's stories unfold is downright unbearable. Because we can't possibly know how their stories will end, their failures are all the more acute, immediate and treacherous; more Shakespearean tragedy than quaint anecdote.

When my children make mistakes that endanger their own happy endings, the bottom drops out of my world, and in those moments there's nothing I'd like more than to be able to flip to the end of their story and reassure myself that everything turns out okay. Sadly, that's not how parenting works. We don't have access to spoilers, and we can't skim through the uncomfortable chapters in our children's story arcs in order to skip to the happy ending. Worse, we can't even know if there will *be* a happy ending.

What we can do, however, is be patient, and trust in our kids. As I watch my own children follow dreams that I may not even be around to witness, I have no choice but to focus on the details of their journey. They are writing their own stories, in their own voices, with plot points of their own invention. Their narrative is not mine, and I can't edit them into perfection. The author Richard Russo wrote, "Great books are not flawless books," and he's right. In order for my children to become masterpieces, their flaws must be allowed to remain, and serve as an essential part of their tale.

ACKNOWLEDGMENTS

Writing may be a solitary endeavour, but the publication of a book is a mass effort. There's no possible way to thank every person who helped transform a late-night idea for a blog post into a book.

The next morning, in between teaching English and Latin classes, that blog post morphed into an article, and K. J. Dell'Antonia suggested I submit it for publication somewhere. Around lunchtime, *Pound Foolish* author Helaine Olen supplied me with Jennie Gritz's email address at the *Atlantic*. By the end of the day, Jennie had accepted, edited, and posted the article "Why Parents Need to Let Their Children Fail." These three women changed the trajectory of my life, and no matter how many times I thank them, it will never be enough.

A good editor is hard to find, and yet I have been fortunate to work with many: K. J. Dell'Antonia at the *New York Times*, Jennie Gritz, Eleanor Barkhorn Britton, Heather Horn, James Hamblin, Ashley Fetters, Julia Ryan, and Emma Green at the *Atlantic*, Betty Smith at Vermont Public Radio, and Cassie Jones

Morgan at William Morrow.

The editor who laboured over this particular book deserves more than a full paragraph of thanks, but she would inevitably make me omit what she would interpret as repetitive and unnecessary sentiments. So thank you, Gail Winston. Thank you. You are a wise and wonderful woman.

When I became a professional writer, I dreaded meeting those territorial, underhanded, catty women writers I'd heard so much about. It seems it's past time to kick that tired stereotype to the curb. These brilliant women have been nothing but kind and generous with their time, quotes, advice, and support: Carol Blymire, Marilyn-Price Mitchell, Michele Borba, Katie Hurley, Andrea Nair, Betsy Lerner and her FTF Writers, Jacoba Urist, Jennifer Hartstein, Christine Gross-Loh, Jennifer Senior, Ashley Merryman, Isabel Kallman, Lisa Belkin, Lisa Heffernan, Launa Schweizer, Naomi Shulman, Kimberly Williams, Jeanne Eschenberg Sager, Catherine Newman, Galit Breen, Aviva Rubin, Laura Vanderkam, Asha Dornfest, Blair Koenig, Amy Gutman, Alicia Ybarbo Zimmerman, Julie Cole, Nancy Rappaport, Jennifer Senior, Gretchen Rubin, Catherine Newman, Priscilla Gilman, Annie Murphy Paul, Kendall Hoyt, Holly Korbey, Avital Norman

Nathman, Sarah Buttenwieser, Megan Rubiner Zinn, Melissa Atkins Wardy, Naomi Shulman, Sue Scheff, Elizabeth Green, Kay Wills Wyma, Ruth McKinney, Kristen Laine, Lisa Damour, Susan Cain, Joanne Wyckoff, Joanne Jacobs, and so many others. I promise to be horrified and embarrassed when I realise my omissions.

And no, I have not forgotten about the boys. Huge thanks to

Robert Pondiscio, my first editor on matters educational. I could not have had a more able and wise mentor. Thanks also to

A. J. Jacobs, Jim Collins, Tom Ryan, John Tierney, Mike Winerip, Paul Tough, Jay Mathews, Greg Toppo, Smoker Shulman, Jeff Valence, Michael Petrilli, K. C. Potts, Don Cannon, Zach Galvin, Dan Willingham, John Boger, Alexander Russo, Larry Ferlazzo, Jordan Shapiro, Matthew Levey, Nikhil Goyal, Ron Lieber, and Scott Barry Kaufman.

Thanks to all the parents, teachers, and students who shared their stories with me. I could not have written this book without you.

To the Writerdinner ladies: K. J. Dell'Antonia, Sarah Stewart Taylor, Sarah Pinneo, Jenny Bent, and Sarina Bowen, thank you for listening to my fears and shoring up my hopes.

Thanks to the Laheys and the O'Haras, family by marriage and temperament. I could not have in-lawed myself to a more loving and supportive cast of characters.

Thanks to my students at the Duke Talent Identification Program, Rowland-Hall/St. Mark's School, Highland High School, Hanover High School, Crossroads Academy, and Valley Vista. You have made me a better educator, writer, parent, and human being.

Thanks to the staff of Crossroads Academy, who supported me when I suddenly and unexpectedly morphed from teacher to teacher/writer.

Thanks to Victoria Pipas for giving over her summer to do some painfully boring administrative grunt work when the demands of writing this book eclipsed just about everything.

Thanks to my agent, Laurie Abkemeier, for continuing to

answer my emails, read my queries, and share my hope that someday, somehow, we would have the chance to work together.

Thanks to my mom and dad, who let me have my autonomy, encouraged me to become a competent human being, and reminded me that they loved me, no matter what my grade, point total, high score, or salary turned out to be.

Finally, thanks to my husband, Tim Lahey, because I'm the lucky one in this equation.

NOTES

17   **trend that's been rising for decades** "A Rising Share of Young Adults Live in Their Parents' Home," August 14, 2013, http://www.pewsocialtrends.org/2013/08/01/a-rising-share-of-young-adults-live-in-their-parents-home/.

27   **most of them children** Steven Mintz, *Huck's Raft: A History of American Childhood* (Cambridge, MA: Harvard University Press, 2004), 15.

27   **"do not instruct children"** Paula S. Fass and Mary Ann Mason, ed., *Childhood in America* (New York: New York University Press, 2000), 45.

28   **"title and right to it"** Ibid., 47.

29   **"keeping up the distinction too long."** Mintz, *Huck's Raft*, 52.

31   **"useful to useless"** Viviana Zelizer, *Pricing the Priceless Child*, (New York: Basic Books, 1985), 56.

33   **"psychologising of childrearing"** Mintz, *Huck's Raft*, 219.

36   **"during adolescence"** Ibid., 316.

40   **"How will I know if I am a good parent?"** "The Top 10 Concerns of New Parents," accessed January 1, 2014, http://www.parent-ing.com/article/the-top-10-concerns-of-new-parents?page=0,0.

49   **"sad state of apathy"** Edward Deci, *Why We Do What We Do: Understanding Self-Motivation* (New York: Penguin), 31.

49   **Detrimental** Ibid., 31.

50   **not given any choice** Ibid., 33.

55   **"falls short of their vision"** Anne Sobel, "How Failure in the Classroom Is More Instructive than Success," *Chronicle of Higher Education*, accessed May 5, 2014, http://chronicle.com/article/How-Failure-in-the-Classroom/146377/.

60   **more is always possible through effort and personal development** Carol Dweck, *Mindset: The New Psychology of Success* (New York: Ballantine, 1978), 6–7.

60   **"persist in the face of obstacles"** Carol Dweck, *Self-Theories: Their Role in Motivation, Personality, and Development* (New York: Psychology Press, 2000), 1.

62   **"desirable difficulties."** Peter C. Brown, Henry L. Roediger III, and Mark A. McDaniel, *Make It Stick: The Science of Successful Learning* (Cambridge, MA: Harvard University Press, 2014), 69.

70   **"striking"** Wendy S. Grolnick, *The Psychology of Parental*

Control: How Well-Meant Parenting Backfires (New York: Psychology Press, 2003), 16.

87   **"It just takes effort"** Christine Gross-Loh, *Parenting Without Borders* (New York: Avery, 2013), 106.

90   **"telling them they were smart"** Carol Dweck, *Mindset: The New Psychology of Success* (New York: Ballantine Books, 2006), 73.

105   **"lack of purpose"** L. L. Harlow, M. D. Newcomb, and P. M. Bentler, "Depression, Self-derogation, Substance Abuse, and Suicide Ideation: Lack of Purpose in Life as a Meditational Factor," *Journal of Clinical Psychology* 42, no. 1 (January 1986): 5–21.

119   **"time unproductively spent"** Hara Estroff Marano, *A Nation of Wimps: The High Cost of Invasive Parenting* (New York: Broadway Books, 2008), 257.

125   **when they witness the emotional healing** Patrick T. Davies, Robin L. Myers, and E. Mark Cummings "Responses of Children and Adolescents to Marital Conflict Scenarios as a Function of the Emotionality of Conflict Endings," *Merrill-Palmer Quarterly* 42, no. 1 (1996).

140   **"Somewhere along the line"** Louis M. Profeta, "Your Kid and My Kid Are Not Playing in the Pros," April 7, 2014, http://www.dgi-wire.com/your-kid-and-my-kid-are-not-playing-in-the-pros/.

141   **"place others' perspectives and needs on a par with their own"** Richard Weissbourd, *The Parents We Mean to Be* (Boston: Mariner Books, 2009), 146.

142   **"The ride home from games with my parents."** Steve Henson,

"What Makes a Nightmare Sports Parent," February 15, 2012, http://www.thepostgame.com/blog/more-family-fun/201202/what-makes-nightmare-sports-parent.

144   **"won a spot in the school orchestra"** Wendy Grolnick and Kathy Seal, *Pressured Parents, Stressed-Out Kids* (Amherst, NY: Prometheus Books, 2008), 26.

144   **"remain close to us and to succeed"** Ibid., 27.

145   **"undermines intrinsic motivation"** Daniel Pink, *Drive: The Surprising Truth About What Motivates Us* (New York: Riverhead Books, 2009), 174.

145   **caused those mothers to overparent** Grolnick, *Pressured Parents*, 99.

150   **"only more struggle"** Michael Thompson, *The Pressured Child: Freeing Our Kids from Performance Overdrive and Helping Them Find Success in School and Life* (New York: Ballantine Books, 2004), 106.

174   **"careers and social interactions"** L. M. Padilla-Walker and L. J. Nelson, "Black Hawk Down?: Establishing Helicopter Parenting as a Distinct Construct from Other Forms of Parental Control during Emerging Adulthood," *Journal of Adolescence* 35 (2012): 1177–90.

176   **"until we are teenagers"** David Bainbridge, *Teenagers: A Natural History* (Vancouver: Greystone Books, 2009), 132.

192   **invite them into the process** Joyce L. Epstein, *School, Family, and Community Partnerships: Preparing Educators and Improving*

Schools (Philadelphia: Westview Press, 2011), 39–40.

213   less than that wreaks havoc on concentration, memory, learn-
        ing, attention, executive functioning, and behaviour "How
        Much Sleep Do I Need?," Centers for Disease Control and Pre-
        vention, accessed July 1, 2013, http://www.cdc.gov/sleep/about_
        sleep/how_much_sleep.htm.

230   "the one who is examined" Ibid.

235   "boosting their achievement" Deborah J. Stipek and Kathy Seal,
        Motivated Minds: Raising Children to Love Learning (New York:
        Holt, 2001), 179.

238   "stay out of the game" Ken Bain, *What the Best College Students
        Do* (Cambridge, MA: Harvard University Press, 2012), 119–20.

243   "Great books are not flawless books" Mary McDonagh Murphy,
        ed., *Scout, Atticus & Boo: A Celebration of Fifty Years of To Kill a
        Mockingbird* (New York: Harper, 2010), 170.

BIBLIOGRAPHY

Adkins, Elaine K. *How to Deal with Parents Who Are Angry, Troubled, Afraid, or Just Plain Crazy.* Thousand Oaks: Corwin Press, 1998.

Alsop, Ronald. *The Trophy Kids Grow Up: How the Millennial Generation Is Shaking Up the Workplace.* San Francisco: Jossey-Bass, 2008.

Anderegg, David. *Worried All the Time: Overparenting in an Age of Anxiety and How to Stop It.* New York: Free Press, 2003.

Apple, Rima D. *Perfect Motherhood Science and Childrearing in America.* New Brunswick: Rutgers University Press, 2006.

Ariely, Dan. T*he (Honest) Truth About Dishonesty: How We Lie to Everyone—Especially Ourselves.* New York: Harper Perennial, 2012.

Arnott, Alastair. *Positive Failure.* Cambridge: Cambridge Academic, 2013.

Bain, Ken. *What the Best College Teachers Do.* Cambridge: Harvard University Press, 2004.

Bainbridge, David. *Teenagers: A Natural History.* Vancouver: Greystone Books, 2009.

Barnes, Christie. *The Paranoid Parents Guide: Worry Less, Parent Better, and Raise a Resilient Child.* Deerfield Beach: Health Communications, 2010.

Bender, Yvonne. *The Tactful Teacher Effective Communication with*

Parents, Colleagues, and Administrators. White River Junction: Nomad Press, 2005.

Berman, Robin E. *Permission to Parent: How to Raise Your Child with Love and Limits*. New York: Harper Wave, 2014.

Bohlin, Karen E., Deborah Lynn Farmer, and Kevin Ryan. *Building Character in Schools Resource Guide*. San Francisco: Jossey-Bass, 2001.

Borba, Michele. T*he Big Book of Parenting Solutions: 101 Answers to Your Everyday Challenges and Wildest Worries*. San Francisco, CA: Jossey-Bass, 2009.

Borba, Michele. *12 Simple Secrets Real Moms Know: Getting Back to Basics and Raising Happy Kids*. San Francisco: Jossey-Bass, 2006.

Brafman, Rom. *Succeeding When You're Supposed to Fail: The 6 Enduring Principles of High Achievement*. New York: Three Rivers Press, 2011.

Brighton, Kenneth L. *Coming of Age: The Education and Development of Young Adolescents: A Resource for Educators and Parents*. Westerville: National Middle School Association, 2007.

Bronson, Po, and Ashley Merryman. *NurtureShock: New Thinking about Children*. New York: Twelve, 2009.

Bronson, Po, and Ashley Merryman. *Top Dog: The Science of Winning and Losing*. New York: Twelve, 2013.

Brooks, Robert B., and Sam Goldstein. *Nurturing Resilience in Our Children: Answers to the Most Important Parenting Questions*. Chicago: Contemporary Books, 2003.

Brown, Dave F., and Trudy Knowles. *What Every Middle School Teacher Should Know. 2nd ed.* Portsmouth: Heinemann, 2007.

Brown, Peter C., Henry L. Roediger III, and Mark A. McDaniel. *Make It Stick: The Science of Successful Learning*. Cambridge: Harvard University Press, 2014.

Cairns, Warwick. *How to Live Dangerously: The Hazards of Helmets, the Benefits of Bacteria, and the Risks of Living Too Safe*. New York: St. Martin's Griffin, 2009.

Campbell, Joseph. *The Hero with a Thousand Faces. 2d ed.* Princeton: Princeton University Press, 1972.

Clark, Ron. *The Essential 55: An Award-winning Educator's Rules for Discovering the Successful Student in Every Child.* New York: Hyperion, 2003.

Clark, Ron. *The Excellent 11: Qualities Teachers and Parents Use to Motivate, Inspire and Educate Children.* New York: Hyperion, 2004.

Coburn, Karen Levin, and Madge Lawrence Treeger. *Letting Go: A Parents' Guide to Understanding the College Years.* 4th ed. New York: Quill, 2003.

Cohen, Harlan. *The Naked Roommate: For Parents Only.* Naperville: Source Books, 2012.

Coles, Robert. *The Moral Intelligence of Children.* New York: Random House, 1997.

Coombs, Loni. *"You're Perfect—" and Other Lies Parents Tell: The Ugly Truth about Spoiling Your Kids.* Los Angeles: Bird Street Books, 2012.

Cooper-Kahn, Joyce, and Laurie Dietzel. *Late, Lost, and Unprepared: A Parents' Guide to Helping Children with Executive Functioning.* Bethesda: Woodbine, 2008.

Csikszentmihalyi, Mihaly. Flow: *The Psychology of Optimal Experience.* New York: Harper & Row, 1990.

Cushman, Kathleen, and Laura Rogers. *Fires in the Middle School Bathroom: Advice for Teachers from Middle Schoolers.* New York: New Press, 2008.

Cutler, William W. Parents and Schools: *The 150-year Struggle for Control in American Education.* Chicago: University of Chicago Press, 2000.

Damon, William. *Greater Expectations: Overcoming the Culture of Indulgence in America's Homes and Schools.* New York: Free Press, 1995.

Deci, Edward L. *Why We Do What We Do: Understanding Self-Motivation.* New York: Penguin Books, 1995.

Dewey, John. *Experience & Education.* New York: Touchstone, 1938.

Duckworth, Eleanor Ruth. *"The Having of Wonderful Ideas" & Other Essays on Teaching & Learning.* New York: Teachers College Press, 1987.

Duhigg, Charles. *The Power of Habit: Why We Do What We Do in Life and Business.* New York: Random House, 2012.

Dunnewold, Ann, and Sandi Kahn Shelton. *Even June Cleaver Would Forget the Juice Box: Cut Yourself Some Slack (and Still Raise Great Kids) in the Age of Extreme Parenting.* Deerfield Beach: Health Communications, 2007.

Dweck, Carol S. Mindset: *The New Psychology of Success.* New York: Random House, 2006.

Dweck, Carol S. *Self-theories: Their Role in Motivation, Personality, and Development.* Philadelphia: Psychology Press, 1999.

Eagleman, David. Incognito: *The Secret Lives of the Brain.* New York: Pantheon Books, 2011.

Elkind, David. *The Hurried Child: Growing Up Too Fast Too Soon.* Reading, MA: Addison-Wesley Pub., 1981.

Epstein, Joyce Levy. *School, Family, and Community Partnerships Preparing Educators and Improving Schools. 2nd ed.* Boulder: Westview Press, 2011.

Epstein, Robert. *The Case against Adolescence: Rediscovering the Adult in Every Teen.* Sanger: Quill Driver Books, 2007.

Esquith, Rafe. *Real Talk for Real Teachers: Advice for Teachers from Rookies to Veterans: "No Retreat, No Surrender"* New York: Penguin Group, 2013.

Faber, Adele, and Elaine Mazlish. *How to Talk So Kids Will Listen & Listen So Kids Will Talk.* New York: Scribner, 1980.

Fass, Paula S. *Childhood in America.* New York: New York University Press, 2000.

Fay, Jim, and David Funk. *Teaching with Love & Logic: Taking Control of the Classroom.* Golden: Love and Logic Press, 1995.

Feldman, David B., and Lee Daniel Kravetz. *Supersurvivors: The Surprising Link between Suffering and Success.* New York: HarperCollins, 2014.

Fried, Robert L. *The Passionate Learner: How Teachers and Parents Can Help Children Reclaim the Joy of Discovery.* Boston: Beacon Press, 2001.

Fried, Robert L. *The Passionate Teacher: A Practical Guide.* Boston:

Beacon Press, 1995.

Friedman, Hilary Levey. *Playing to Win: Raising Kids in a Competitive Culture*. Berkeley: University of California Press, 2013.

Galinsky, Ellen. *Mind in the Making: The Seven Essential Life Skills Every Child Needs*. New York: HarperStudio, 2010.

Gardner, Howard, Mihaly Csikszentmihalyi, and William Damon. *Good Work: When Excellence and Ethics Meet*. New York: Basic Books, 2001.

Gawande, Atul. *The Checklist Manifesto: How to Get Things Right*. New York: Metropolitan Books, 2010.

Gill, Tim. *No Fear: Growing Up in a Risk Averse Society*. London: Calouste Gulbenkian Foundation, 2007.

Ginsburg, Kenneth R., with Martha Moraghan Jablow. *Building Resilience in Children and Teens: Giving Kids Roots and Wings*. 2nd ed. Elk Grove Village: American Academy of Pediatrics, 2011.

Ginsburg, Kenneth R., and Susan FitzGerald. *Letting Go with Love and Confidence: Raising Responsible, Resilient, Self-sufficient Teens in the 21st Century*. New York: Avery, 2011.

Glenn, H. Stephen, and Jane Nelsen. *Raising Self-reliant Children in a Self-indulgent World: Seven Building Blocks for Developing Capable Young People*. Rocklin: Prima Publishing & Communications, 1988.

Goldberg, Donna. *The Organised Student: Teaching Children the Skills for Success in School and Beyond*. New York: Fireside, 2005.

Goleman, Daniel. *Focus: The Hidden Driver of Excellence*. New York: HarperCollins, 2013.

Gray, Peter. *Free to Learn: Why Unleashing the Instinct to Play Will Make Our Children Happier, More Self-reliant, and Better Students for Life*. New York: Basic Books, 2013.

Grolnick, Wendy S. *The Psychology of Parental Control: How Well-meant Parenting Backfires*. Mahwah, N.J.: L. Erlbaum Associates, 2003.

Grolnick, Wendy S., and Kathy Seal. *Pressured Parents, Stressed-out Kids: Dealing with Competition While Raising a Successful Child*. Amherst: Prometheus Books, 2008.

Gross-Loh, Christine. *Parenting without Borders: Surprising Lessons Parents around the World Can Teach Us.* New York: Avery, 2013.

Harford, Tim. Adapt: *Why Success Always Starts with Failure.* New York: Picador, 2011.

Hartley-Brewer, Elizabeth. *Talking to Tweens: Getting It Right before It Gets Rocky with Your 8- to 12-Year-Old.* Cambridge: Da Capo Press, 2005.

Hays, Sharon. *The Cultural Contradictions of Motherhood.* New Haven: Yale University Press, 1996.

Hazard, Kris. *The Hazard of the Game: The Dangers of Over-Parenting in Sport and Life.* North Word Communication, 2012.

Heath, Ralph. *Celebrating Failure: The Power of Taking Risks, Making Mistakes, and Thinking Big.* Pompton Plains: Career Press, 2009.

Hodgkinson, Tom. T*he Idle Parent: Why Laid-back Parents Raise Happier and Healthier Kids.* New York: Tarcher Penguin, 2009.

Hoefle, Vicki. *Duct Tape Parenting: A Less Is More Approach to Raising Respectful, Responsible, and Resilient Kids.* Brookline: Bibliomotion, 2012.

Holt, John. *How Children Fail.* New York: Da Capo Press, 1982.

Homayoun, Ana. *That Crumpled Paper Was Due Last Week: Helping Disorganised and Distracted Boys Succeed in School and Life.* New York: Penguin Group, 2010.

Honoré, Carl. *Under Pressure: Rescuing Our Children from the Culture of Hyper-parenting.* New York: HarperOne, 2008.

Hulbert, Ann. *Raising America: Experts, Parents, and a Century of Advice about Children.* New York: Vintage, 2003.

Icard, Michelle. *Middle School Makeover: Improving the Way You and Your Child Experience the Middle School Years.* Brookline: Bibliomotion, 2014.

Kahn, Joyce, and Laurie C. Dietzel. *Late, Lost and Unprepared: A Parents' Guide to Helping Children with Executive Functioning.* Bethesda: Woodbine House, 2008.

Kaufman, Scott Barry. *Ungifted: Intelligence Redefined: The Truth about Talent, Practice, Creativity, and the Many Paths to Greatness.* New York: Basic Books, 2013.

Kilpatrick, Haley, and Whitney Joiner. *The Drama Years: Real Girls Talk about Surviving Middle School: Bullies, Brands, Body Image, and More.* New York: Free Press, 2012.

Klee, Mary Beth. *Core Virtues: A Literature-based Program in Character Education,* K–6. Redwood City: Link Institute, 2000.

Koenig, Blair. *STFU Parents: The Jaw-dropping, Self-indulgent, and Occasionally Rage-inducing World of Parent Overshare.* New York: Perigree, 2013.

Kohn, Alfie. *Punished by Rewards: The Trouble with Gold Stars, Incentive Plans, A's, Praise, and Other Bribes.* Boston: Houghton Mifflin, 1993.

Kohn, Alfie. *What Does It Mean to Be Well Educated?* Boston: Beacon Press, 2004.

Lareau, Annette. *Unequal Childhoods: Class, Race, and Family Life.* 2nd ed. Berkeley: University of California Press, 2011.

Lawrence-Lightfoot, Sarah. *The Essential Conversation: What Parents and Teachers Can Learn from Each Other.* New York: Ballantine, 2003.

Lee, Ellie, Jennie Bristow, Charlotte Faircloth, and Jan MacVarish. *Parenting Culture Studies.* Hampshire: Palgrave Macmillan, 2014.

Levine, Alanna. *Raising a Self-reliant Child: A Back-to-basics Parenting Plan from Birth to Age 6.* Berkeley: Ten Speed Press, 2013.

Levine, Madeline. *Teach Your Children Well: Parenting for Authentic Success.* New York: Harper, 2012.

Levine, Madeline. *The Price of Privilege: How Parental Pressure and Material Advantage Are Creating a Generation of Disconnected and Unhappy Kids.* New York: HarperCollins, 2006.

Levine, Mel. *A Mind at a Time: America's Top Learning Expert Shows How Every Child Can Succeed.* New York: Simon and Schuster Paperbacks, 2002.

MacDonald, Betty Bard. *Mrs Piggle-Wiggle.* Philadelphia: J. B. Lippincott Company, 1947.

Magary, Drew. *Someone Could Get Hurt: A Memoir of Twenty-first Century Parenthood.* New York: Gotham Books, 2013.

Marano, Hara Estroff. *A Nation of Wimps: The High Cost of Invasive*

Parenting. New York: Broadway Books, 2008.

Mathews, Jay. *Work Hard. Be Nice: How Two Inspired Teachers Created the Most Promising Schools in America.* Chapel Hill, NC: Algonquin Books of Chapel Hill, 2009.

McArdle, Megan. *The Up Side of Down: Why Failing Well Is the Key to Success.* New York: Viking, 2014.

McEwan, Elaine K. *How to Deal with Parents Who Are Angry, Troubled, Afraid, or Just Plain Crazy.* Thousand Oaks: Corwin Press, 2005.

Medina, John. *Brain Rules: 12 Principles for Surviving and Thriving at Work, Home, and School.* Seattle, WA: Pear Press, 2008.

Mintz, Steven. *Huck's Raft: A History of American Childhood.* Cambridge: Harvard University Press, 2004.

Mogel, Wendy. *The Blessing of a B Minus: Using Jewish Teachings to Raise Resilient Teenagers.* New York: Scribner, 2010.

Mogel, Wendy. *The Blessing of a Skinned Knee: Using Jewish Teachings to Raise Self-reliant Children.* New York: Scribner, 2001.

Nelson, Margaret K. *Parenting out of Control: Anxious Parents in Uncertain Times.* New York: New York University Press, 2010.

Nichols, ML. *The Parent Backpack for Kindergarten through Grade 5.* Berkeley: 10 Speed Press, 2013.

Payne, Kim John, and Lisa M. Ross. *Simplicity Parenting: Using the Extraordinary Power of Less to Raise Calmer, Happier, and More Secure Kids.* New York: Ballantine Books, 2009.

Payne, Ruby K. *Working with Parents: Building Relationships for Student Success.* Highlands: Aha! Process, 2006.

Peskowitz, Miriam. *The Truth behind the Mommy Wars: Who Decides What Makes a Good Mother?* Emeryville: Seal Press, 2005.

Phelan, Thomas W. *Surviving Your Adolescents: How to Manage and Let Go of Your 13–18 Year Olds.* 3rd ed. Glen Ellyn: ParentMagic / EBL, 2012.

Pincus, Donna. *Growing up Brave: Expert Strategies for Helping Your Child Overcome Fear, Stress, and Anxiety.* New York: Little, Brown and, 2012.

Pink, Daniel H. Drive: *The Surprising Truth about What Motivates Us.* New York: Riverhead Books, 2009.

Quart, Alissa. Hothouse Kids: *The Dilemma of the Gifted Child.* New York: Penguin Press, 2006.

Reichert, Michael, and Richard A. Hawley. *Reaching Boys, Teaching Boys: Strategies That Work and Why.* San Francisco: Jossey-Bass, 2010.

Rosenfeld, Alvin A., and Nicole Wise. *The Over-scheduled Child: Avoiding the Hyper-parenting Trap.* New York: St. Martin's Griffin, 2001.

Sarkett, John A. *Extraordinary Comebacks: 201 Inspiring Stories of Courage, Triumph, and Success.* Naperville: Source Books, 2007.

Savage, Marjorie. *You're on Your Own (but I'm Here If You Need Me): Mentoring Your Child during the College Years.* New York: Fireside Book, 2003.

Schipani, Denise. *Mean Moms Rule: Why Doing the Hard Stuff Now Creates Good Kids Later.* Naperville: Source Books, 2012.

Schwartz, Natalie. T*he Teacher Chronicles: Confronting the Demands of Students, Parents, Administrators and Society.* Millwood: Laurelton Media, 2008.

Senior, Jennifer. *All Joy and No Fun: The Paradox of Modern Parenthood.* New York: Ecco, 2014.

Shumaker, Heather. *It's OK NOT to Share.* London: Penguin Books, 2012.

Siegel, Daniel J. Brainstorm: *The Power and Purpose of the Teenage Brain.* New York: Penguin, 2013.

Silverman, Scott, ed. *How to Survive Your Freshman Year. 5th ed.* Atlanta: Hundreds of Heads Books, 2013.

Skenazy, Lenore. *Free Range Kids: How to Raise Safe, Self-reliant Children (without Going Nuts with Worry).* San Francisco: Jossey-Bass, 2010.

Smallwood, Mary Lovett. *An Historical Study of Examinations and Grading Systems in Early American Universities.* Cambridge: Harvard University Press, 1935.

Spar, Debora L. *Wonder Women: Sex, Power, and the Quest for Perfection.* New York: Sarah Crichton Books, 2013.

Stearns, Peter N. *Anxious Parents: A History of Modern Childrearing in America*. New York: New York University Press, 2003.

Steinberg, Laurence. *Age of Opportunity: Lessons from the New Science of Adolescence*. New York: Houghton Mifflin Harcourt, 2014.

Steinberg, Laurence D., and Ann Levine. *You and Your Adolescent: A Parent's Guide for Ages 10 to 25*. New York: Harper & Row, 1990.

Stipek, Deborah J., and Kathy Seal. *Motivated Minds: Raising Children to Love Learning*. New York: H. Holt and, 2001.

Taylor, Jim. *Positive Pushing: How to Raise a Successful and Happy Child*. New York: Hyperion, 2002.

Thompson, Michael. *Homesick and Happy: How Time Away from Parents Can Help a Child Grow*. New York: Ballantine Books Trade Paperbacks, 2012.

Thompson, Michael, and Teresa Barker. *The Pressured Child: Helping Your Child Find Success in School and Life*. New York: Ballantine Books, 2004.

Thompson, Michael, Lawrence J. Cohen, and Catherine O Grace. *Mom, They're Teasing Me: Helping Your Child Solve Social Problems*. New York: Ballantine Books, 2002.

Thompson, Michael G., and Alison Fox Mazzola. *Understanding Independent School Parents: The Teacher's Guide to Successful Family-School Relationships*. Wise Teacher Press, 2012.

Tingley, Suzanne Capek. *How to Handle Difficult Parents: A Teacher's Survival Guide*. Fort Collins, CO: Cottonwood Press, 2006.

Tobias, Cynthia Ulrich. *I Hate School: How to Help Your Child Love Learning*. Grand Rapids: Zondervan, 2004.

Tough, Paul. *How Children Succeed: Grit, Curiosity, and the Hidden Power of Character*. Boston: Mariner Books, 2012.

Tulgan, Bruce. *Not Everyone Gets a Trophy: How to Manage Generation Y*. San Francisco, CA: Jossey-Bass, 2009.

Twenge, Jean M. *Generation Me: Why Today's Young Americans Are More Confident, Assertive, Entitled—and More Miserable than Ever Before*. New York: Free Press, 2006.

Twenge, Jean M., and W. Keith Campbell. *The Narcissism Epidemic: Living in the Age of Entitlement.* New York: Free Press, 2009.

Ungar, Michael. *Too Safe for Their Own Good: How Risk and Responsibility Help Teens Thrive.* Crows Nest: Allen & Unwin, 2008.

Ungar, Michael. *The We Generation: Raising Socially Responsible Kids.* Cambridge, MA: Da Capo, 2009.

Vuko, Evelyn Porreca. *Teacher Says: 30 Foolproof Ways to Help Kids Thrive in School.* New York: Perigee Books, 2004.

Wagner, Tony, and Robert A. Compton. *Creating Innovators: The Making of Young People Who Will Change the World.* New York: Scribner, 2012.

Walsh, David Allen, and Nat Bennett. *Why Do They Act That Way? A Survival Guide to the Adolescent Brain for You and Your Teen.* New York: Free Press, 2004.

Walsh, David Allen. *No: Why Kids—of All Ages—Need to Hear It and Ways Parents Can Say It.* New York: Free Press, 2007.

Warner, Judith. *Perfect Madness: Motherhood in the Age of Anxiety.* New York: Riverhead Books, 2006.

Weissbourd, Rick. *The Parents We Mean to Be: How Well-intentioned Adults Undermine Children's Moral and Emotional Development.* Boston: Houghton Mifflin Harcourt, 2009.

Wilde, Jerry. *An Educator's Guide to Difficult Parents.* New York: Kroshka Books, 2000.

Willingham, Daniel T. *Why Don't Students like School?: A Cognitive Scientist Answers Questions about How the Mind Works and What It Means for the Classroom.* San Francisco: Jossey-Bass, 2009.

Wiseman, Rosalind, and Elizabeth Rapoport. *Queen Bee Moms & Kingpin Dads: Dealing with the Parents, Teachers, Coaches, and Counselors Who Can Make—or Break—Your Child's Future.* New York: Crown Publishers, 2006.

Wood, Chip. *Yardsticks: Children in the Classroom, Ages 4–14: A Resource for Parents and Teachers. Expanded ed.* Greenfield: Northeast Foundation for Children, 1997.

Wyma, Kay Wills. *Cleaning House: A Mom's 12-month Experiment to*

Rid Her Home of Youth Entitlement. Colorado Springs: WaterBrook Press, 2012.

Zelizer, Viviana A. Rotman. *Pricing the Priceless Child: The Changing Social Value of Children.* New York: Basic Books, 1985.

"It's hard to overstate the importance of this book. *The Gift of Failure* is beautifully written; it's deeply researched; but most of all it's the one book we all need to read if we want to instil the next generation with confidence and joy."
Susan Cain, author of *Quiet*

"'Failure-avoidant' parenting would seem, on the surface, to be synonymous with good parenting. Lahey proposes, however, that parents will ultimately serve their children better by allowing them to stand on their own abilities and experience failure... Lahey has many wise and helpful words – ones that any parent can and should embrace."
Publishers Weekly

"Finally an antidote to all the hysteria! Through an artful combination of anecdote and research, Lahey delivers a lesson that mums and dads badly need to learn and secretly wish to hear: that failure is vital to children's success. Any parent who pines for a saner, more informed approach to childrearing – to say nothing of a sounder night's sleep – should read this book. "
Jennifer Senior, author of *All Joy and No Fun*

Kristin Hobermann

Jessica Lahey is an American teacher and writer.
She writes the bi-weekly "Parent-Teacher
Conference" advice column for the *New York Times*
and is a contributing writer at the *Atlantic*.
She currently teaches English and writing, but
retains a special place in her heart for Latin.
She lives in New Hampshire with her
husband and two sons.